INDETERMINACY

DISCOURSE 006

INDETERMINACY
Thoughts on Time,
the Image, and Race(ism)

David Campany &
Stanley Wolukau-Wanambwa

7 INTRODUCTION

   PART ONE
11 The perils of representation
17 Refusal and fugitivity
24 Fixity, slippage, and indeterminacy
40 Fabulation, fragmentation, and the freeze frame

   PART TWO
59 The itinerant image
65 Blurred lines
69 Margin as foundation

   PART THREE
77 A question of time(liness)
86 Seeing, contingency, and embodiment
92 Against the spectacular

97 INCONCLUSION

INTRODUCTION

'Art expands the sympathetic imagination while teaching us about the limits of sympathy. […] There is no formula, however, for aesthetic education of this kind […] It is rarely prescriptive, and, although it may schematize itself as a set of rules (as a poetics or a hermeneutics), the type of thinking involved seems to import a structural moment of indeterminacy that escapes the brain's binary wiring. A sort of unframed perception becomes possible, a suspension or confusion of personal identity.'

Geoffrey Hartman[1]

A free-flowing exchange could well be the ideal form to explore indeterminacy. We cannot say we knew this when we began to share thoughts with each other via email, but we must have intuited it, and somewhere along the line we must have become more conscious of the fact that the form our writing was taking was well suited to what was, and is, on our minds.

The title of this book came late in the day. It was only when looking back that we realised how much it had to do with the indeterminate nature of the photograph. For those interested in the image, particularly the photographic image, indeterminacy is always to be reckoned with, aesthetically and politically. What is at stake in its essential ambiguity, its mobility of meanings and affects? How is the relation between a photograph's fixed appearance and its unfixed meaning to be understood? How are relations between urgent resistance and photographic indeterminacy to be grasped and explored, critically and creatively?

In book form, our exchange unfolds at the steady rhythm of pages. The reality of its writing was much more intermittent. It began with a conversation prompted by David's book and travelling exhibition *a Handful of Dust*.[2] Indeterminacy was at the heart of that project, which took a speculative look at the poetics and politics of what can happen when a wide range of tangentially related images are placed in each other's orbit. David is a curator and writer while Stanley is an artist and writer, but we both share an interest in what photographs can and cannot disclose, what they suggest, what they might claim, and how they are less knowable than we may wish or need them to be.

That first exchange shaped the contours of our subsequent discussions to some extent, sharpening our thoughts and opening some possibilities. Our conversation continued over the summer of 2020, with David recently moved to the United States, where Stanley had been based for some time. The country had lurched further towards fascism, with all the racist violence that entailed. In addition, it was suffering the tragic consequences of a catastrophically mishandled pandemic. In this context we were moved to ask: What places does the photographic image have in moments of crisis? Is its utility premised on a capacity to overcome its indeterminacy? Is it a matter of putting the image 'to work'? Or are there valuable dimensions of indeterminacy to hold onto?

Our ongoing exchange became a matter of trying to think things through in the midst of unpredictability and danger, our noses pressed against history as it unfolded. Writing always affords some measure of distance, particularly in the essay form that we both hold dear. But an exchange has a different dynamic, a different pulse, and a good one can feel more like a snapshot than a distant contemplation. Yes, the text was revised for publication, clarified and fleshed out here and there, but in essence it is a record of thoughts shared on the fly and in the moment – a mutual effort to understand the changing shape of our historical present.

1   Geoffrey Hartman, 'Tele-Suffering and Testimony in the Dot Com Era', in *Visual Culture and The Holocaust* ed. by Barbie Zelizer (London: The Athlone Press, 2001), pp. 122–123.

2   David Campany, *a Handful of Dust* (London: MACK, 2015); 'a Handful of Dust', curated by David Campany, Le Bal, Paris, (18 October 2015 – 31 January 2016).

PART ONE

The perils of representation

Stanley Wolukau-Wanambwa: One thing that has had the most consequential impact on my thinking over the last five years has been my engagement in the theory coming out of the field of Black studies.[3] What I've found there is a transformative confrontation with modernity as a fundamentally racist and racialising enterprise. I've found a confrontation with the force and effect of economies of desire in the elaboration of hegemonic, normative categories of being, or accounts of law and reason – none of it easily reducible in any way to a simplistic celebration of cultural difference. Identity is such an amenable host for the exploitative forces of neoliberal capital. It can abet the perception that representation *within* capital equates to value, and perhaps to safety within its embrace. We can get intensely (over) invested in those representations.[4] What Black studies has helped clarify for me is how the production of racial difference as such is inseparable from the violent, expropriative agenda of capitalism, and that the notionally whole autonomous individual subject sits at the centre of this morass.

What I've found empowering in Black studies is its exploration of the potency (and the threat) that subaltern practices cultivate from their positions of abjection: the ways of living with a different concept of value as members of the value-less, the ways of eluding and refusing conceptual capture within the hegemonic order of racial capital by embracing a position of exteriority, by doing away with the ostensible universality of 'reason' or 'civility'.[5] We saw some part of this broader politics of *refusal* evidenced in the extraordinary sweep and depth of protest and outrage, of unrest and assembly happening in the US and globally in the summer of 2020.

But the image, this thing we both love and work with, seems to have had so much success as an implement for ratifying the presence of those who have historically been marginalised (or, for that matter, for anyone who feels they are not being sufficiently heard or seen). This makes it such a tricky thing to deal with in this context, especially when *appearance* (as a product and profit centre of corporate media) can itself power and extend the dominant reach of the forms of neoliberal hegemony that undergird the racial and economic order we see people protesting today.

David Campany: I moved to the United States recently, from the UK. I cannot help but be struck by the often glaring chasm between identity politics and anti-capitalism ('notional disciplinary isolation' is itself political), and the

Kimberly Jones, 'How can we win?', YouTube, May 2020

way in which images – which always show but without being able to account for what they show – are often what determine public debate. Just after I arrived, Covid-19 hit and it was immediately apparent that it was going to affect the poor disproportionately, and since the poor are disproportionately non-white, there would be a profound racial disparity in the impact of the virus. The appalling death toll grew. The callous – and racist – indifference of the Trump administration was costing tens of thousands and then hundreds of thousands of lives.

Very slowly, in April and May of 2020, it felt as if public debate was edging towards a proper engagement with the crisis. It seemed that, for the first time in quite a while, questions of race and class, race and economy, would be discussed in relation to each other at a national level (if not in government) as fundamental to the situation. But the debate didn't seem to quite take hold, and neither did the public outrage. I suspected it had something to do with the absence of images. It really shouldn't have had anything to do with images, but I suspected it did. Covid-19 is invisible, and its effects are insidious. It's not easy to picture. Various public commentators noted this absence from the visual register. What images we had were graphs, statistics, and the picturing of an emptying out. Vacant streets. Social distancing. No images of deaths in obscene numbers.

And then something shocking and focused happened. George Floyd was violently killed by a white police officer. And it was filmed. Video and audio. The imagery is horrifying and horrifyingly familiar. And Floyd's words were just as powerful. 'I can't breathe.' (In the weeks prior I had been thinking that the anger against Trump's mishandling of Covid-19, if it didn't have an iconography, could do with a slogan at least, and 'I can't breathe' might have been an effective one, given that this is how the virus kills.) But Covid-19 was proving too abstract to rally around, not quite socially specific enough to rally around, and not visual enough. George Floyd's killing was extremely visual and extremely racial. Had it not been filmed, the waves of anger and frustration with racial injustice may not have swelled quite as they did.

Thomas Prior, *Untitled, New York City*, 2020, from *Amen Break* (2020)

In the civil rights and worldwide anti-colonial movements of 1968, and in their immediate legacies, the connection between racism and the 'expropriative agenda of capitalism' was understood quite clearly and with a historical grounding. Think of Martin Luther King arguing that:

> Capitalism does not permit an even flow of resources. With this system, a small privileged few are rich beyond conscience, and almost all others are doomed to be poor at some level. That's the way the system works. And since we know that the system will not change the rules, we are going to have to change the system.[6]

The imperatives of colonial capitalism and slavery produced a pernicious racial order as a means of justification for its violence. A decade later however, the ascent of neoliberalism with its credo of free markets and the self above all drove a wedge between politics and what came to be called identity politics. It was a wedge that the left was very slow to see for what it was (I have found Michael C. Dawson's writings and his podcast *New Dawn* to be informative on this matter).

Indeed, much of the left was already ahead of the game (or behind), becoming so preoccupied with representation at the level of the image that it often mistook it for political representation. This was pure ideology (as a student of both Marxism and psychoanalysis I learned that ideology is the merely symbolic resolution of real contradiction). Being represented in an image doesn't mean you are represented in any other way. Being imaged is vital, for sure, not least as a kind of currency in visual culture, but we will still have the political struggle ahead of us. Two people may struggle for representation at the level of the image but they *may* have no more in common politically than that. The image itself, self-imaging, participating in the circulation of imagery, cannot alone constitute a form of justice. Or if it does constitute a form of justice, it is most readily equated with the demand for a seat at the neoliberal table, in the hope of 'comfort in its embrace', as you put it. And neoliberalism had already implied, quite self-servingly and disingenuously, that the most efficient form capitalism can take is that of an equal-opportunity exploiter. 'Yes, this was a system built upon slavery, and the appalling social and psychical effects of that are still with us,' it seems to say, 'but it is working towards a position where it doesn't care what colour you are, who you sleep with or in what position, or what superstitious beliefs comfort you. The most efficient capitalism cares only for those in power and it

Michael C. Dawson, *Behind the Mule: Race and Class in African-American Politics* (1995)

doesn't even care about *their* identity.' That is its mythology. Obviouslywe mustn't delude ourselves that if it wasn't racist, sexist, and homophobic, the neoliberal order would somehow be fair. The fight for fairness is a fight against capitalism. All this to say, if one concludes that racism is structural to capitalism, it commits anti-racism to anti-capitalism, and vice-versa (and in the end one cannot 'commit' to an 'anti-', but to a 'pro-'). This was a difficult question somewhat dodged by the Obama administration, and with grave consequences, I think.

SW-W: It's hard for me to envision a form of capitalism that can sacrifice anti-Blackness or structural racism more broadly, simply because value and autonomy and sovereignty and property are concepts wholly saturated by race and racial difference. Without them, you don't have a logic or a set of affects with which to rationalise and mobilise capitalist desire and production. Do you see a really or notionally colourless version of capitalism afoot? Does it materialise or coalesce in images?

DC: No, I don't, but I'm aware there are other views. Perhaps I wasn't being quite clear there. I suspect it is neoliberalism's *own* self-justifying narrative that suggests there is such a thing as post-racial, and post-patriarchal capitalism.

3   See: Hortense Spillers, Sylvia Wynter, Saidiya Hartman, Angela Y. Davis, Denise Ferreira da Silva, Tina Campt, Elizabeth Alexander, Krista Thompson, Christina Sharpe, Crystal Nicole Feimster, Rizvana Bradley, Simone Browne, Leigh Raiford, Kimberly Juanita Brown, Alexander Weheliye, Jared Sexton, Roderick Ferguson, C. Riley Snorton, David Marriott, Frank B. Wilderson III, Stefano Harney & Fred Moten, among many others.

4   Darby English writes: 'In the 1960s blacks became, through their own hard cultural work, the representatives and representations they had sought in vain from a reluctant, at times unspeakably hostile white American mainstream. If the counterpositive integrity of the affirmative image proved especially compelling, it is because it is a good that at any moment can be brought about now.' 'How It Looks to Be a Problem', *1971: A Year in the Life of Color* (Chicago: University of Chicago Press, 2016), p. 93.

5   Kyla Wazana Tompkins and Tavia Nyong'o, 'Good Morning 1877, Sit Down: On Civility, Reconstruction, and our Revanchist Moment', *Capacious: Journal for Emerging Affect Inquiry*, 1:3 (2018) <https://capaciousjournal.com/cms/wp-content/uploads/2018/10/capacious-tompkins-and-nyongo-good-morning-1877.pdf>

6   Martin Luther King, quoted in Harry Belafonte, *My Song: A Memoir of Art, Race and Defiance* (Edinburgh: Canongate Books, 2012), p. 328

Refusal and fugitivity

DC: I'm interested in what you said about subaltern strategies, and strategies of exteriority. Are these ways of refusing the terms offered by the dominant regime of the image, the image under neoliberalism? Ways of finding other relations to or with images?

SW-W: In this moment, one of those strategies that I know that I, and a number of other Black artists and thinkers are employing is to refuse to make ourselves available and visible in certain spaces, to get together and plan off to the sides of things, and to be strategic about the conditions and terms within which we might return – temporarily, because these upwellings have a history of subsiding – to the centre. The iceberg economies of Black gathering and thought are a place in which exteriority is claimed as a kind of potent resource, and those practices have many histories, but if you think of the figure of the hold in the slave ship, they also have real structural causes too.

George Floyd's lynching – which is what I think it has to be defined as – marks the contours of the limits imposed upon Black bodies in some complicated ways: he is in his car, which, in the US, constitutes sacrosanct space, but he is denied that interiority by the arresting officers, one

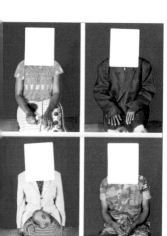

Tina M. Campt, *Listening to Images* (2017)

of whom immediately draws a gun to compel him to exit the vehicle, whereupon he can be wrestled to the ground at the point of a gun, and denied the right to safely occupy public space either. So appearance, exteriority, these things are profoundly differentiated positions to take up for Black people under white supremacy, since the image – *the appearance of Blackness* – can by itself constitute a threat to which lethal violence is a legitimate response.

I love the #IfTheyGunnedMeDown Tumblr, which I discovered in Tina Campt's fantastic book *Listening to Images*.[7] I think that this Tumblr constitutes a kind of subaltern practice that engages the complex conditions of appearance for Black people in the United States. It started as a hashtag on twitter, and then became a Tumblr archive that continues to expand, and its central premise is simple: what image would the media and the state use to define me if they gunned me down? That image is counterposed with another image that fundamentally contradicts the anticipated choice that the media and the state would make. So the images are anticipatory descriptions of the future abjection and dismissal of unarmed, innocent future Black dead. They're dying declarations, in the words of Languid Hands.[8] Those future deaths are envisioned and claimed in the present. To borrow from Roland Barthes's *Camera Lucida* (with which I have very real beef), each participant in the series 'observe[s] with horror an anterior future of which death is the stake.'[9] Campt writes of them:

> Refusing to wait passively for a future posited as highly likely or inevitable for black urban youth, the sitters actively anticipate their premature deaths through these photos. In doing so, they enact anterior practices of fugitivity through their refusal to be silenced by

the probability of a future violent death they confront on a daily basis. Through these images they fashion a futurity they project beyond their own demise.[10]

Interestingly, the antagonist image to the racist trope each participant shares very often centres a kind of professionalism, a kind of fitness for civil society, a competence in negotiating the neoliberal market that implicitly seems to say: I am a fit and proper current or future member of your institutions. The kind of professionalism that is opposed to the 'abject' image of Blackness is typically grounded in

ejmartinez, image from 'If They Gunned Me Down', Tumblr

educational accomplishment, in seemly appearance, in membership of the institution of family, in governmental or military service to the nation, in a kind of corporate refinement – in a kind of aspiration to participation in normativity, one way or another. This doesn't leave much room for a set of important critiques that refuse 'innocence' as a precondition for care in instances of Black death at the hands of the state. Jackie Wang has written a fantastic essay about this, called 'Against Innocence: Race, Gender, and The Politics of Safety' that I highly recommend, and I think that in a different way David Marriott's complicated and rich essay 'On Decadence: *Bling Bling*' also drives at the distinction between reformist and radical Black politics of resistance.[11] There's an important discussion there precisely about the need for an anti-racist politics to also be an anti-capitalist politics, and Marriott and Wang both clarify this persuasively and emphatically. The idea, in their work, cannot be to *fit in* but to collectively *break out*. But for me, these images' relevance stems from the fact that these image-making practices accurately index the casual impossibility of claiming a right to rights as a Black person in the United States, and their temporality, their envisioning of an exhausted futurity 'beyond their own demise' is extraordinarily powerful.

One of the most notable and long-lasting effects of seeing Kerry James Marshall's extraordinary retrospective 'Mastry' in 2017, was, for me, the apprehension that the precise features of his Black subjects eluded solid distillation in my mind: I couldn't hold on to them as images.[12] If you try and remember the full dimensions of the human face in those portraits, it's easy to remember the figure, the pose, the colour, but I'd argue that the specificity of the human faces he paints is in some way unfixable – deliberately *undefined* – and that has everything to do with how he mobilises Blackness in his work. That too constitutes a resistant aesthetic practice with a clear political history *and* effect. We can easily extend that thought to Roy DeCarava, and think more about secrecy and shadow, or about refusal and fugitivity as Tina Campt describes them, as part of the complex bargain that Blackness has to make with the visible.

DC: Where Kerry James Marshall achieves that unfixability at the level of paint, Roy DeCarava arrived at something similar through the specifics of photographic exposure, chemistry, and printing. Many of his images seemed to push expectations of visibility and visuality, expectations of the photographic rendering of Black bodies. And like Marshall's paintings, DeCarava's photographs are almost impossible to reproduce on the page in all their nuance. It makes the impact of seeing them in exhibition all the more profound and rich. It means the work of these artists doesn't really circulate in the cultural economies of reproduction, at least not very satisfactorily, and it is interesting to think of this through the terms of exteriority and refusal as you just described them.

SW-W: I think that's exactly right: there's something evanescent about their richness that cannot be relayed and reliably reproduced within the given parameters of image circulation that undergird and power the capital markets of art acquisition. It likely matters not at all to most buyers and sellers, to the extent that they are only interested in trade. What I think I'm always interested in is the possibility of slipping intruder agents nakedly through the front door, and in that sense, I think that Black aesthetic strategies of refusal, Black practices of fugitivity manage to effect this extraordinarily complex act of giving and *at the same time* taking away. It's right there in DeCarava and Marshall, but also in Deana Lawson's extraordinary portraits.

I think of Lawson because of the delicate and powerful way in which she bonds together on the one hand interiority and domesticity with, on the other, formality and austere restraint, so that these diametrically opposing valences of intimacy and withdrawal ground so many of her frames. Her interior portraits blend these phenomena in a practice that seems to extend an invitation to all of us outsiders who see the portraits to enter deeply and freely into the permeable and violable space of Black domesticity. And yet, the formality of her portraiture, the physical withdrawal, or *recession* into the frame on the part of many of her subjects is rigorously impersonal and militates against any romantic notion that the pictures might give us not only access to but rights to possess what is shown.[13] When I wrote about the work recently, I suggested that 'we are permitted to enter, but we are not invited to stay', and I think that that refusal of an elision of access with *rights* is so vital to a portrait practice grounded in the space of Black domesticity.[14] Breonna Taylor's murder proves, yet again, that traditional American notions of autonomy and sovereignty over domestic space simply are not and cannot be extended to sites of Black gathering – this was so painfully articulated in the murder of Botham Jean – and I think that all of these tensions intersect or traverse the raced body in richly complicated ways.

DC: One of the things at stake here, and you phrase it well in relation to Deana Lawson's work, is that the portrait photograph, perhaps now more than ever, functions as both a frustrated promise of revelation (of interior life) and as a form of cultural currency that signifies and circulates without need of such revelation. Lawson's brilliance, a disturbing brilliance I think, is that ability to keep these pressures in tension. Are we being granted an insight into the inner life and specificity of her sitters, or are these images best understood as interventions in the rhetoric of Black portraiture? That tension is always there in the photographic portrait made public, but in the current moment in culture Lawson's adept handling of it produces quite extraordinary intensity. It's a radical indeterminacy, although I notice a lot of the commentary that swirls around her work does not quite address or accept this, and forces itself into singular claims on the work's behalf. That's not unique to Lawson; I think the skirting around radical indeterminacy is a problem in cultural commentary at large right now, but specifically in relation to photography (a medium that is fundamentally indeterminate). I know this is something you and I share, in our thought and writing: this need to keep open what is undecidable, against the pressure to make this or that affirmative 'reading'.

7   Tina M. Campt, *Listening to Images* (Durham, NC: Duke University Press, 2017); #IfTheyGunnedMeDown, Tumblr, <https://iftheygunnedmedown.tumblr.com/>
8   Languid Hands is an artistic and curatorial collaboration, which consists of Rabz Lansiquot and Imani Robinson. See: <https://languidhands.co.uk/>

9   Roland Barthes, *Camera Lucida: Reflections on Photography* trans. by Richard Howard (New York: Hill & Wang, 1981), p. 96.

10   Campt, *Listening to Images*, p. 109.

11   Jackie Wang, 'Against Innocence: Race, Gender and The Politics of Safety', *LIES Journal*, 1 (2014) <https://www.liesjournal.net/volume1-10-againstinnocence.pdf>; David Marriott, 'On Decadence: Bling Bling', *e-flux Journal*, 79 (February 2017) <https://www.e-flux.com/journal/79/94430/on-decadence-bling-bling/>

12   Kerry James Marshall, 'Mastry', The Met Breuer, New York, 25 October 2016 – 29 January 2017.

13   See: Stanley Wolukau-Wanambwa, 'Spectacular Opacities', *e-flux Journal*, 120 (September 2021) <http://worker01.e-flux.com/pdf/article_416942.pdf>

14   Stanley Wolukau-Wanambwa, 'Black Stars', *Dark Mirrors* (London: MACK, 2021), p. 247.

Fixity, slippage,
and indeterminacy

DC: Intriguingly, with her book of portraits published in 2018, Deana Lawson makes reference to the famous Diane Arbus publication of 1972. Both books were published by Aperture and both are subtitled *An Aperture Monograph* (Lawson's revival of the wording is explicit). Moreover, among Lawson's portraits there is an image of what looks like a peeling photographic mural of a landscape. It is uncannily similar to a photograph in the Arbus book, which actually contains three such images of fake facades, strategically scattered through the sequence of portraits almost as cautionary reminders: *all a photograph offers you is light bouncing first off the surface of whatever was before the camera, and then off the surface of the print or page. And those surfaces can be deceptive, untrustworthy, not what they seem, less than they seem, or more than they seem. A photograph cannot explain what it shows, cannot disclose intention with any confidence.* It would be tempting to ask Lawson about her thoughts and intentions here, and I'm sure they're fascinating, but there's more to be gained from thinking for oneself than from deferring to the artist's account.

What you say takes me back to writing my first book, *Art and Photography*, in 2002.[15] I remember trying to think through the various conflicting forces in photographic portraiture, for makers, subjects and viewers: the promise of revelation,

Spreads from *Diane Arbus: An Aperture Monograph* (1972) and *Deana Lawson: An Aperture Monograph* (2018)

opacity, withdrawal, refusal, as a sort of semiotic strategy. I don't think I would have put it in quite those terms to myself back then, but still. Post-conceptual art, postcolonial theory and feminism had in their different ways pushed portraiture if not into crisis, then into a position where its status in and as art had to be, in one way or another, a conspicuously reflexive questioning of what a portrait is and does. That happened for reasons internal to art, but also in response to the increasing reduction of identity *to* image in visual culture more broadly. So my focus was on Cindy Sherman, Thomas Ruff, Ken Lum, Ajamu X, Rotimi Fani-Kayode, Faisal Abdu'Allah, Roni Horn, Jo Spence, and not Diane Arbus, or Peter Hujar, or Roy DeCarava. Were I to rewrite that book now, I probably would include images by those latter names, while looking to draw out the deeper continuities between them all.

It is very difficult to avoid the seductions of the portrait – its promises of interior life; its default use as a passport into consumer capitalism; its reifications of consciousness and selfhood; its reduction of identity to a legible brand in the attention economy, and so forth. I'm interested in how fugitivity and refusal might lead to a decision not to represent bodies, one's own or others, but to come at the question indirectly. Clearly the visual is enormously determinant in a racialised and imagistic society. Race signals itself at the level of the body's exterior and to that extent the visual plays a major part in the constitution, fixing and unfixing of subjectivities. And yet no one but the narcissistic really wants to be judged by appearance. What's most interesting about most of us as people may have little to do with our appearance. That's not to deny the given stakes of visibility, but it is to challenge them. Looking through your various projects, on pages and on walls, written and photographic, I sense you coming at this question from a number of directions, sometimes deflecting away from the body; sometimes turning bodily performativity for the camera in on itself, or against itself, almost as if quoting or allegorising it, but, in general, never allowing the photograph to present itself in plenitude, as a full account of embodied subjectivity. You're interested in the picturing of subjectivity in flight, peeling off, eluding capture, permitting it to be visualised only obliquely, or *en abyme*. Plus, of course, many of your photographs addressing the body and its conditions do not picture bodies at all.

SW-W: That's an incredibly generous and attentive reading of my work. I suspect (although my account of what influences me should itself be suspected) that growing up Black in hegemonically white societies has played a central role in what you're describing in my work. The entry point for the essay at the end of my book *One Wall a Web* is a composite narrative of many experiences I had as a child both in Zimbabwe and in England, in which I learned that this body that was notionally 'mine' didn't in fact belong to me at all, and was traversed by and organised in response to a set of forces wholly external to it.[16] I wouldn't have been able to describe my apprehension of this in those terms obviously, but I can remember numerous instances and sensations that very clearly articulated that my Black body was the subject *of* others, or a menace *to* others, or an exotic rarity *for* others even before it was 'my own', and so I think I started to learn how to modulate and organise it in relation to those forces. This would have been an integral part of the process of learning how mimicry and performance serve as essential processes in the formation and extension of a 'self' in the world. While these dynamics are by no means exclusive to me, or to Black people, the necessity of accommodating oneself to them consciously (and, as a matter of survival) does not fall evenly across all differences, least of all for an African kid going to a virtually all-white school in England.

One of the things I had to learn how to do really quickly after arriving in England was lose my thick Zimbabwean accent, and pick up a raft of colloquialisms that were expressly English and not African. Doing so was a matter of survival, and so I think I was compelled to think early and often about the partiality and contingency of the 'I' that I was, or the vulnerability of the body that 'I owned'. Growing up in those sorts of schools was in many ways a constant repeating circuit of violent disruptions of the illusion that any parts of myself were fully mine, and at the same time an intense course of study in all the ways that the 'I' that I was or am is always contextual and contingent and reactive, and never stably self-identical. Of course these were lessons administered almost exclusively through the tutelage of pain, in one way or another, but something of the truth they materialise certainly stayed with me.[17] I think that it informed the way that I watched other people growing up, and that that likely informs my interest in portraiture as well. I think that those experiences certainly attuned me toward those instances in the archival photographs I collected in which the depicted person seems to be struggling to accommodate themselves to the demands of the performance imposed upon them by the attentions of the camera, or the people that surround them as the camera makes their picture. Part of one's emergence into subjecthood, and the extent to which that emergence is conflictual, is a function of one's accommodation to or refusal of the obligation to perform according to those scripts.

DC: There is a fascinating exchange between the critic Benjamin Buchloh and the photographer Thomas Struth in which Buchloh wants to suggest that the Pop portraits of Andy Warhol mark the beginnings of the neoliberal order in which the demands of the camera are equated with the demands of the marketplace – the positionings, brandings and commodifications of selves and subjectivities according to its warp. I'm interested in what you say about the struggle to accommodate the demands of the image, and also the refusal to accommodate, depicted within the realm of the image itself. In these scenarios the photograph presents subjectivities that are not fully present, awkwardly present, elusively present, inadvertently present, confusingly or ambivalently present. Selves and subjects are seen slipping through the grasp of the camera. It's a strategy, if we can even call it that, which keeps the door open both to other kinds of photography and other kinds of selfhood, beyond restrictive expectations and coercions.

SW-W: That's the beautiful thing about the photograph – the way that it always arrives to us in the mode of deferral: a not quite, a not yet, a not nearly, a not *all the way*. But I agree that there's a way to slip the symbolism and registers of plenitude and self-identity in a portrait, and I think that for some – perhaps for many people – there's something oddly sacrilegious about having an avowed commitment to documentary practice, and yet being interested in a kind of portraiture that reflexively signals its arbitrary impositions *and* the difficulties that people have in accommodating themselves to the strictures that the photograph imposes. Reflexivity is notionally conceptual, and by the laws of mutual exclusion, indexicality is documentary – if I can briefly counterpose those two terms. I know that these are distinctions that can't be solidified into effective organising terms – photographs are too messy for this sort of clear mapping – but what's funny is that I was thinking of, say, MoMA's 1922 palladium print of *Rebecca* by Paul Strand as an instance of the indexical, and immediately thought of his *Blind Woman, New York* (1916) as a perfect instance of the reflexive. The point being that these emphases, these inflections, were never mutually exclusive agents in documentary form, but somehow the reality (and even the *realisms*) of contingency are harder to accept when we're after a document's capacity to produce facts. Truth has always been multifold, but photography has contributed to the expectation that it be fixed and singular.

This notion of the honorific in portraiture practice extends far beyond art, and in histories of photography it arguably originates in other related but distinctly capitalist practices that used art as cover for competitive advantage in the burgeoning marketplace of modern life. Allan Sekula's essay *The Body and the Archive* is lurking in the wings here, as is John Tagg's *A Democracy of the Image*, but I think so too is the visual economy of social media, and the way that perhaps the most ubiquitous and widely consumed image form in social life is the selfie.[18] It's funny how much Instagram now does the work that Southworth & Hawes did in the nineteenth century.[19] I mention this to point out that my attraction to a portraiture that unwinds the expectation of stable self-identity, and that destabilises expectations of the image's correlation with the fullness of an interior life is

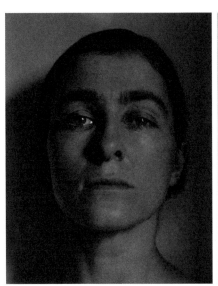

Paul Strand, *Rebecca*, 1922; Paul Strand, *Blind Woman, New York*, 1916

likely antagonistic to those image practices, and to the performances that ratify their norms.

It seems to me that a desire for continuous self-identity and an enduring, transhistorical sameness is a deeply territorial and corporate kind of desire – an imperious and imperial claim that reflects a deep fear of contingency and the messiness of human interaction. So if one *can* love a portraiture of slippage, then maybe that opens the door for a changed relationship to the self as well. I feel quite differently now about portraiture than I did when I made the earliest work in *One Wall a Web*, and I think that the portraits in the earliest work that still have a strong hold on me are those that ask questions of themselves as legibly (and problematically) as they stipulate the physical presence of others in the image's depiction. I guess I want both mirror *and* window.

Stanley Wolukau-Wanambwa, *Officer Earl Miller, posing with the revolver used in the suicide of sixteen year-old Peter Lo Dolce, a student of Lane Tech, in the apartment of his fifteen year old classmate, Carmen Salanir, on June 24th 1951, Chicago, IL,* from the series *All My Gone Life* (2014–16)

DC: Does this mean a particular kind of image, or a particular deployment of it that might keep things open and unsettled for a viewer?

SW-W: I think that at times I'm interested, within portraiture, in a kind of picture that describes a pose that questions what its photographed image might performatively bring into being, because there's something of that inchoate questing uncertainty about *how to be* that makes subjecthood so fraught. At one and the same time, I'm also interested in cultivating an awareness in a viewer of the circuitry of appetitive consumption by way of which we can consume other people as images,

Stanley Wolukau-Wanambwa, *W. Baker Street*, 2014, from the series *Our Present Invention* (2012–14)

and so I'm after a kind of picture that elicits that desire but fails to readily consummate it. I think that I want it to be difficult for someone to have a settled relationship to the images that I produce. But I have realised these last few years in particular, living in the United States, that a tremendous amount of my imagination is trained on the instants *immediately preceding action* in the sight of the other, since those are the final fractions of a second open to me as a Black male in the United States. I can't help but think that that likely also has some influence on my engagement with portraiture, but as I said earlier on: I'm likely not the most trustworthy narrator of the things driving my attachments and obsessions.

DC: It's fascinating to look at earlier moments of resistance to mainstream portraiture. In 1936, Helmar Lerski made *Metamorphosis Through Light*, which is such a provocative body of work. Lerski was of the view that there really

is no correspondence at all between outward appearance and inner being, inner life, character. A head or face is merely a socially and psychologically charged surface that can be illuminated and photographed in an infinite number of ways. Lerski met a man in Palestine, who he photographed around 175 times. Just his face, each time lit and framed differently. Light is bouncing around via multiple angled mirrors (Lerski had a background in expressionist cinematography). By the time you have looked at the entire series you have a lot of ideas as to what this person may have 'really' looked like but no sense at all of the person. It's endlessly descriptive and endlessly deferring; disturbing, but strangely liberating.

Lerski projected some of these portraits (if that's even the word for them) as a slideshow in a movie theater, but the series wasn't published until the 1980s. In 1931 he did publish *Köpfe des Alltags* (*Everyday Heads*), a book which seemed to undermine the typological and honorific approach to portraiture that was being made by August Sander at that time.[20] Lerski's contents page lists various professions, just like Sander's book *Antlitz der Zeit* (*Face of the Time*, 1929): Porter, Baker, Secretary, Banker, Farmer, and so on. But Lerski offers three or four radically divergent images of each person, not just one. The viewer cannot can not get a 'fix' on the sitters, who are permitted to elude the camera's classificatory protocols, and its tendency to reduce a person to their place in society.

Of course, Sander's project is much celebrated, and easier to comprehend almost a century on, while Lerski's was so at odds with the emerging visual culture in which, as Walter Benjamin put it in his well-known remarks about Sander's book, 'Whether one is of the Left or the Right, one will have to get used to being looked at in terms of one's provenance. And one will have to look at others the same way.'[21] Lerski's work was largely forgotten but there has been much renewed interest, which I'm inclined to read in parallel to this resistance to the hegemonic, authoritarian, and branding tendency of the portrait photograph.

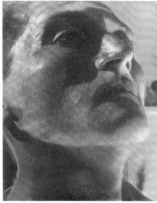

Helmar Lerski, photographs from the series *Metamorphosis Through Light* (1936)

The camera is *always* 'othering' what it pictures. We tend to think of othering as a dynamic rooted in power relations – ideologies, discourses, and institutions. The 'male gaze', the 'colonial gaze', and so on. There's often a presumption that if we got rid of those then photography would be set free along with its subjects. There is some truth in this, and much urgency too, but it won't get us around photography's unavoidable and inevitable othering which will always be operative above and beyond, or below and beyond, the power relations that might put it to work. I get the impression that debates around photographic representation today are edging towards a reckoning with this. The deferral to photographers' intentions as the script for the viewer's looking is a frustrating symptom of it: an attempt to reassure the viewer, in the face of their uncertainty and confrontation, with an othered and unknowable portrayal, that the image is 'coming from a good place', that it is well-intended. But that's just a stop-gap, really, and it doesn't get us to the essential ambiguities of the photograph, and the essential othering of the apparatus, of the photographic act itself. Photography presents selves without consciousness, and invites the psychological projection of the viewer.

In a similar vein to Lerski, I think of the staged photographic illustrations made by Gordon Parks for *Life* magazine, of moments from Ralph Ellison's first-person novel *Invisible Man* (1952). For a long time, the celebrated image from that series was of the Black writer/protagonist of the novel emerging from, or disappearing under a manhole cover. More recently, however, it's been the image of him alone in his basement, backlit by all those light bulbs, with his record player and notepads. It's the scene of writing as described in the novel's prologue. The writer has set up home in a windowless basement sequestered from a white society that barely sees him as a person. But he is present to himself in all that light (hotwired from the building above), and he is in the process of writing what you are about to read, an episodic but epic novel about what it is to be a Black man in post-war America. Parks portrays him in not-quite silhouette, on the cusp between being an individual and a broader symbol or cypher.

Ellison's prologue also inspired a photograph by Jeff Wall in 1999/2000. Wall was unaware of Parks's precedent, but it's interesting that he faced the same pictorial challenge, opting not for back-lighting, but for what French art history calls the 'profil perdu': he is turned away but we see just enough of his face to register him as an individual. Moreover, in both interpretations of the scene we get the fantastical existential conundrum of the photographic depiction of a moment of complete aloneness, supposedly beyond the gaze of others. A novelist can describe a character in isolation, but a photographer cannot, or cannot *quite*, because the fact of the present camera implies an observer (even a self-portrait photograph does this, since it externalises the self and the camera as other). So these images have a suspended, dreamlike quality, in which the camera's documentary description is at odds with the fictive status of the scene. Again, I think the current interest in such images is, in a roundabout way, related to these questions of fugitivity, refusal, and suspension.

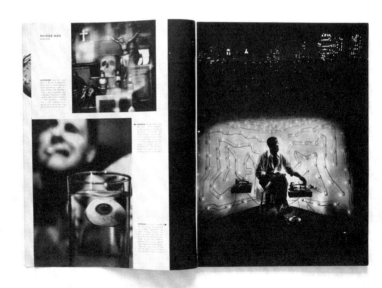

Spreads from Gordon Parks and Ralph Ellison, 'A Man Becomes Invisible', *Life*, 25 August 1952

Jeff Wall, *After "Invisible Man" by Ralph Ellison, the Prologue*, 1999–2000

Can you say a little about the image we've chosen for the cover of this book? It's from your collection of vintage press photo negatives bought online.

SW-W: It's one of the images that I've often shown in public talks, and on one occasion used as a poster to promote a talk.

I tend to show it in the talks without the caption, and in my book, *One Wall a Web*, the caption is quite far removed from the image. In exhibition, I would similarly separate caption from image as much as is practicable to delay the reading of the visual through the framing of the verbal, but here they're brought together more or less immediately. The photograph is one of a number of press photographs, as you say, that seem to have been made on assignment by a photojournalist covering a beat, and picturing noteworthy 'events.' Everything about its framing centres the figure and the plight of the white woman being restrained on this bed as a doctor operates on her bloodied neck. Her face is tensed in a plaintive and deeply pained expression, or so it seems, and her eyes are directed straight at us as viewers, while the attentions of the two nurses whose faces we can see, and of the doctor, are squarely focused on her body. She is, in every sense, the centre of attention.

In most instances when I show this image and ask about people's reactions to it, they begin and end with pain and the plight of the injured woman, and they orbit around the intrusion of the photographer and the question of privacy, or they talk about the use of violence in the production of care. When I then introduce the caption into the conversation, or make it visible, the whole tenor of the conversation shifts, as people begin to reckon with the fact that the woman being operated on was armed and shot by the police. Even then, however, the conversation still tends to centre around her actions, and her role as protagonist in both the frame and the caption tends to overwrite the experiences of everyone else in the photograph.

There's a way that compositional language, interpretive codes we've developed in the captioning of images, and social relations structured by racism and gender all collude in the figuring of her as the principal and essential figure in the action that the photograph describes. That makes a lot of sense to me. But that's merely one way that it can be read. The trouble, of course, is that the ubiquity of such image-interpretive practices make it seem that that is the *only* way to read the image.

I can't help but think about the Hippocratic Oath when I look at it, and even when I first scanned it to see what I had bought, I thought about the perilous work of being a Black medical professional tending to a white woman in such times. I thought about the risks of failure for Black medical staff serving white Americans. In the United States, so much Black and Brown labour is invested in the remediation and preservation of white psychic and bodily integrity, and even a statement like that can be construed as a vicious attack, but such a defensiveness is also the product of reading practices steeped in deep disavowal about racial difference.

I think about the labour being performed in the image, but I also think about what the nurses and doctor might have been thinking – or might have gone on to think – as they

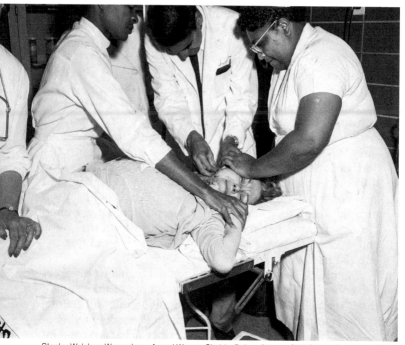

Stanley Wolukau-Wanambwa, *Armed Woman Shot by Police, Chicago (1957)*, from the series *All My Gone Life* (2014–16)

reckoned with the reality that a white woman who shot at the police survived to tell of it, thanks in part to their efforts. For an image suffused by such intense expressions of pain, there really isn't much of any force visible in the hands that restrain her (of which I can only count two). No one seems to be tensed, or using aggressive levels of physical violence to restrain her. To the contrary there's something gentle and precise about the ministrations that surround and attend to her, and yet the binaries of Black and white – as a matter of tone in the image, as a consequence of the intensifications of the camera flash, and as a matter of race and racism in the world – seem to charge the image with a level of absolute, violently differentiated antagonism. I think that those are the perils of binary conceptions of the world, and that we have to find or cultivate a capacity to stay in those combustible conjunctures long enough for the graduated differentiations of life to begin to reveal themselves. In that sense, I think that there's an ethics to an embrace of indeterminacy, and I think that in time – *over* time – photographs can make that manifest, if we'd only listen to them.

15 David Campany, *Art and Photography* (London: Phaidon, 2003).
16 Stanley Wolukau-Wanambwa, *One Wall a Web* (Amsterdam: ROMA, 2018).
17 See: Stanley Wolukau-Wanambwa, 'Picturing Time', in Steve McQueen, *Year Three* (London: Tate, 2022), p. 320.
18 Allan Sekula, 'The Body and the Archive', *Art Isn't Fair: Further Essays on the Traffic in Photographs and Related Media*, ed. by Sally Stein and Ina Steiner (London: MACK, 2020), pp. 99–135; John Tagg, 'A Democracy of the Image: Photographic Portraiture and Commodity Production', *The Burden of Representation: Essays on Photographies and Histories* (Basingstoke: Palgrave Macmillan, 1988), pp. 34–59.
19 See: Robert A. Sobieszek, Odette M. Appel (eds), *The Daguerreotypes of Southworth & Hawes* (New York: Dover Publications, 1980).
20 Helmar Lerski, *Köpfe des Alltags* (Berlin: Verlag Hermann Rockendorf, 1931).
21 Walter Benjamin, 'Little History of Photography', 1931, in *Selected Writings, Part 2, 1931–1934*, ed. by Howard Eiland, Michael William Jennings, and Gary Smith (Cambridge, Massachusetts and London: Harvard University Press, 1999), p. 520.

Fabulation, fragmentation, and the freeze frame

DC: To return to your earlier point, it seems the discussion that really has to happen is around what's at stake in fugitivity and refusal, and also in the embrace via the often manipulative and fixed terms on offer in contemporary culture.

SW-W: I think a certain experience of living otherwise, aligned not just to different principles but to different desires or rhythms is at stake in that choice. I was talking recently about the ways that hip-hop was such a transformative and restorative resource for me in my youth. I think that my body knew certain things about the forms of expression that it afforded me, and the forms of sociality that it made possible that my brain was not yet capable of articulating. I too felt the fracture of being marked as Black when I arrived in Britain from Zimbabwe in 1987, and I too experienced the psychic splintering that Frantz Fanon describes as *epidermalisation*. I think that hip-hop embraces fracture, disjointedness, hybridity, a rhythmic dissonance, an industrial and expressly technological materiality, and its forms of dance provide a means for articulating and exploring that mode of experience as a kind of *power* or a kind of *poesis*. If racialisation introduces fracture and destroys any expectation for bodily and psychic coherence, hip-hop can provide a physiological mode of embracing disjointedness, of embracing the syncopated experiences of the conscious body. I think Mark Fisher is talking about something related in an essay of his called 'The Metaphysics of Crackle: Afrofuturism and Hauntology', about the aesthetics of the sample in music, when he writes:

> If the metaphysics of presence rests on the privileging of speech and the here-and-now, then the metaphysics of crackle is about dyschronia and disembodiment. Crackle unsettles the very distinction between surface and depth, between background and foreground. In sonic hauntology, we hear that time is out of joint. The joins are audible in the crackles, the hiss… The surface noise of the sample unsettles the illusion of presence.[22]

There's something important in this idea of materialising disorder, the sensuous irreducible disordering that music can elicit and produce. So, part of the potency of this is that one need not be Black to embrace fracture, to work toward rejecting a desire for individual autonomy and singularity and separateness and psychic integrity. This presents a challenge to the whole symbolic and politico-economic regime of value that we live under in the US, but that's the insurrectionary potency of the no-thing. Hip-hop makes me want *not* to be reducible to a single autonomous thing, but rather makes me want to embrace hybridity and constant unpredictable transformation. It makes *affectability* a kind of transcendence, and I'd argue that you can see this in the way that people dance to it.

DC: This makes me think again of the Tumblr #IfThey-GunnedMeDown. Such strategies of tense – anticipatory futures, alternative pasts, parallel presents – seem to me increasingly vital, and not least because what we call the present tense is so often prescribed and proscribed, almost hegemonically so. As many have been saying recently, the normal is only normal for a few, and there must be no returning to it. But strategies of tense also point us, in a sort of allegorical way, to the slippage of tense that is implicit in the idea of 'rights'. The moment of the institutionalising

Still from Kendrick Lamar, 'Alright' (2015), directed by Colin Tilley

of rights has to deny its own moment, its own conditionality, in order to propose that rights are timeless, tenseless, universal, that they always already were there, have hitherto been unrecognised but are being recognised now. Accepting this slippage is not to undermine the notion of rights, but it does place the emphasis firmly back on the conditionality of the moment of their declaration. Do rights require a necessary but strategic disavowal of that slippage in tense? In many ways I think subject formation – identity – is always a combination of disavowals, slippages, and strategic refusals. We're certainly starting to see this become apparent in the footholds being gained by the discussions of whiteness as a fraudulently self-serving myth of normativity and wholeness, of the violence implicit in whiteness being proposed and perpetuated as an 'unmarked' term that embodies what counts as normal and complete.

SW-W: I think you're right about the conditionality of rights, and about the kind of slippage that their institutionalisation depends upon, at least in the ways that we live in the white western world. Other practices of collective self-determination are clearly possible, and I think part of what we've seen through Occupy and Ferguson, MO, and the Movement for Black Lives right up to this summer is the development of a set of practices in which people enunciate for themselves the terms according to which they wish to live, in the temporary autonomous zones, right out there in the street. I'd argue that the phrase 'Black Lives Matter' is the emblematic instance in this moment of a declaration seeking the power to be fully performative, and to then acquire a kind of transhistorical power as you say: it's a phrase in search of the right to be an absolute right. And yet, no matter how many times people repeat it, the American state continues to demonstrate, day after day, that in fact Black lives do not matter to it at all.

DC: Psychic integrity – the feeling of wholeness, immanence, completeness, plenitude – is always, from a psychoanalytic point of view, a fantasy. What matters is who gets to believe and inhabit such fantasy, who is denied it, what are the cultural moments of its undoing, and at what moments the undoing (what you describe as the refusal and the strategic no-thing) is generative. For me, some of the most compelling accounts of the debilitating fantasies of race have emerged from psychoanalytic theory. For example, Sheldon George's *Trauma and Race: A Lacanian Study of African American Racial Identity* hinges on the fact that all subjectivity is split, less than whole, internally conflicted, and that one of the most damaging consequences of the racial mindset is that it denies this.[23] It presumes for both oppressor and oppressed fixed and whole subject positions. It leads George to be very suspicious of any emancipatory project that does not recognise this, although he's mindful that it is extremely difficult to mobilise politically around something as radically open-ended as the internally and eternally conflicted psyche. Yet, we see compelling moments – and they can only be moments, not movements – in which the claims for emancipation are grounded in precisely this. George looks to the subjectivities described in the novels of Toni Morrison and Ralph Ellison, for example. Arguably, ambitious culture, important culture, is grounded in the refusal of the fixed terms on offer in favor of keeping

Bill Clark, *Black Lives Matter Plaza*, 5 June 2020

the door open to complexity, provisionality, possibility. It's heartening to see a revival of interest in Stuart Hall's writings on this too.[24] He was always defending nuance in the face of simplification, resisting the strategic essentialisms that might offer short term gains, knowing that in the end complexity is what the struggle needs to be about and over, because it's true.

What I have loved about hip-hop, and still do, is that the great fountains of invention – linguistic, sonic, melodic, and sustained for forty years now – far outstrip its visuals, which in general have played safer and kept it real, rather than radically unreal. In hip-hop's still photography, there has been a preference for visual wholeness, bodily and psychic integrity, and for understandable reasons: the image of confidence and success. The wobble, the jouissance, the moments of radical breakdown, undoing, and unpredictable opening out, are in the music. Arguably sonics and vocals have more access to those registers than the written word and the still image, and I've never been sure what to make of this. Would you agree, and if so where does this leave photography?

SW-W: So much of the capacity to effect material change through performative utterances is contingent upon who is 'speaking thus', to borrow from Abigail Solomon-Godeau.[25] That's part of why I'm glad to see such an intergenerational, international, and multiracial coalition of protest and rebellion in the streets. Elizabeth Alexander, who wrote an extraordinary essay for the catalogue for Thelma Golden's Whitney Museum exhibition 'Black Male: Representations of Masculinity in Contemporary American Art' (1994–5), called 'Can You Be BLACK and Look At This?', has recently written another beautiful text for *The New Yorker*, which ends in a rumination on three hip-hop videos. She says:

> Lamar embodies the energy and the message of the resonant phrase "black lives matter," which Patrice Cullors, Alicia Garza, and Opal Tometi catapulted into circulation when, in 2013, they founded the movement. The phrase was apt then and now. Its coinage feels both ancestral in its knowledge and prophetic in its ongoing necessity. I know now with certainty that there will never be a moment when we will not need to say it, not in my lifetime, and not in the lifetime of the Trayvon Generation.[26]

She's writing about Kendrick Lamar's song, but also about the video for his song.[27] Among that group of three videos, she also cites the filmmaker Khalil Joseph's video for Flying Lotus's song 'Until the Quiet Comes', and I think that they're both examples of a kind of critical Black fabulation that takes flight, fugitivity, fantasy, and decimation very seriously, and that explores the impossibility of wholeness.[28] Joseph's video also considers death and ritual practices in complicated ways, where the ubiquity of Black death is engaged and acknowledged, but death itself is not accepted as a limit. Both videos play with time, with the return of ghosts, with dreams as acts of planning as much as forms of escape – both are about a kind of futurity, and that seems right and proper to the reality Alexander is describing: one in which we will hear again, recursively, the phrase 'I can't breathe' from the lips of yet another dying Black man. This

Still from Flying Lotus, 'Until the Quiet Comes' (2012), directed by Kahlil Joseph

horrifying list, 'Three Words. 70 Cases. The Tragic History of "I Can't Breathe"' recently released by *The New York Times* gives us the echoes of this proleptically I think.[29]

I agree that sound and the moving image have greater access to these sorts of transcendent registers of experience, although I don't think that that means that photographs have no access to them at all. I think the stopped motion of the photograph can provoke a deep and visceral experience for a viewer, and that variously scaled printed objects can interpellate people's bodies into images in really complex and rich ways. Of course, by distinction with cinema and music, those viewing experiences are generally isolated and individuated, which I think bears on their possible intensity.

DC: Still photography has access to those registers, but they are often harder to reach in the face of its fixity. I would agree that there's been far more room to manoeuvre in music videos than photography, and the best of the recent examples are certainly looking to open out spaces of speculative subjectivity.

It's interesting that you mention the 'stopped motion' of the photograph, which points towards the ways that photography might address its own extractedness, its own fragmentary relation to the continuum of life and of the moving image. That's there in Roland Barthes's 'The Third Meaning', an essay on film frames and their ability to radically explode cinema's protocols of looking and interpreting, destabilising spectatorship in the process.[30] This idea got taken up by so many photographic artists from Cindy Sherman, Jeff Wall, and Victor Burgin to Stan Douglas and Mitra Tabrizian. 'Stilledness' is also there in the critiques and avant-garde reimaginings of mainstream cinema, in the work of Agnès Varda, Jean-Luc Godard, Chris Marker, Harun Farocki, and Hito Steyerl (and many more): the freeze frame as a literal and metaphorical way of suspending the cultural habits of moving image consumption, to open out a more critical and reflective space. But 'stilled' photography and 'still' photography are not quite the same thing. Still photography is too often granted the status of being a whole rather than a fragment (leading dangerously to the fetish of the 'iconic' image, which stands in for and obfuscates the contradictions and denials of a situation it purports to summarise). This is probably why most critically minded photographic practices look to the image sequence and to image/text – what Allan Sekula once called the 'disassembled movie'. While not impossible to achieve or access with a single still image, it's much more difficult, I think.

SW-W: Yes. I've been really struck by the power of the stilled image in Rabih Mroué's *The Pixelated Revolution* (2012), which is a lecture performance that has also been condensed into a standalone video, but which has also resulted in a series of 'stills', called *The Fall of a Hair: Blow Ups* (2012).[31] I first saw the works installed in the excellent group show 'Scenes for a New Heritage' at MoMA in summer 2015.[32]

The two pieces pivot around these videos Mroué started finding on Facebook early in the Syrian Revolution, which come from cellphone footage taken by Syrians tracking Assad's troop movements through their cities with their phones. In a terribly large number of these videos, the cameraperson discovers a sniper moving around the city, who then discovers that he is being recorded, pivots, aims and

shoots at the camera, resulting in the wounding, or in many instances apparent death of the people making the record.

In the video, Mroué revisits and slows and stops and reverses and extends these moments, and interrogates the decisions of the two protagonists, and really plumbs the forms of looking and embodied action that they're both engaged with: cameraperson *and* viewer. In the MoMA show, he blew up these freeze frames to 60 in. tall prints, hung with clips from the wall, and they were staged at the far end of a long corridor maybe twenty metres away upon entry, so that at a distance the figures seemed to resolve quite clearly. As you approach the surface of the print, the image dissolves into pixels, and after reading a little about the provenance of the images, you discover that in some cases you've travelled the inverse trajectory of the bullet that stopped the scene unfolding.

So much of the force of the work was held, to my mind, in the tremendous amplitude of everything that's not captured in the image but that sits just outside the frame: the acute contingency of the prints and of the 'cuts' enacted in the footage and on the bodies of the camerapeople; the incompletion that marks the relationship between the footage and the event. These things really charged them as *stilled* images. The prints made corporeity and the capacity to assume the stance of a distanced spectator a kindly fleshly and political quandary to reckon with, against the shimmer of the

Rabih Mroué, *The Fall of a Hair: Blow Ups*, 2012

high-gloss prints and in the funereal black space of the gallery. I
thought about the Maurice Blanchot essay 'The Two Versions
of the Imaginary' and of his notion of being seized by distance when one lives an event as an image.[33] One can be
stilled or stopped by the unbridgeable divide that the image
instantiates as well, and in some sense become its instrument:
another important kind of affectability. Stoppages can be so
powerful, and in photography, where they hinge upon a continuum that somehow forces its way into the frame as an
irredeemable absence, they can create real force.

I wonder, though, whether this is most effective at the
limit case of death, and depictions that directly concern it?
I've also been thinking about practices of holding vigil with
images of this sort, or of assembling in response to the sorts
of care and attention that they call out for. Mroué is very
clear that for Assad, invisibility is of vital tactical necessity.
In the case of George Floyd's lynching, the determination
to violently assert the state's unrestricted right to kill whom-
ever challenges the (white) masculinity of those police officers charged with enforcing the law is nauseatingly theatrical
and spectacular. And of course, so much of what catalyses
the rituals now performed in protest across the US is the
phrase 'I can't breathe'. Differing contexts clearly call for differing responses, but I think those responses are increasingly
deploying the image strategically and publicly in relation

to a political economy, and that they're constituting new aggregates, new publics, however temporary.

DC: I noticed that Graydon Carter penned a bizarre piece in *GQ* magazine that attempts to position an image from the video footage of George Floyd's murder within an already over-familiar history of iconic press images.[34] And yes, you can imagine what those images are: the 'napalm girl', the Kent State shooting, flag raising on Iwo Jima. It's the sinister-banal calendar-flipping version of US history-as-photographs. It's telling that Carter chose nothing from the intervening half century, a period in which still photography was clearly eclipsed from its position at the centre of visual culture. He, or maybe his art director, selects a frame from the video and turns it black and white – so it's a stilling, a desaturation, a classicising, and also a silencing. The video is made less shocking, and more easily assimilable into coffee-table history.

As far back as 1937, Beaumont Newhall, of the Museum of Modern Art, New York, had noted that well-known images of world events were already being derived from moving footage. It's not a new phenomenon at all. But when what is most significant about the footage of George Floyd's killing is its duration (the nine minutes and twenty-nine seconds during which he was choking under the policeman's knee) and the sound of his words ('I can't breathe'), the conversion to a mute still for convenient slotting into a pre-packaged history with terms and criteria not updated for decades is shocking. Yet this dynamic is not at all uncommon. Mainstream media likes the still and mute version of the past, since photographs can be talked over, written over, spoken on behalf of. In other words, they can be put to ideological use. That's not so easy to do with nine minutes and twenty-nine seconds of video.

SW-W: I think this is really tricky. Not the Graydon Carter move, but the underlying current that you point toward. Carter's editorial for *GQ* is strangely (and I'd say meaningfully) muddled in its analysis and description of the American fabric, and the logic that preserves its order. His lament is for an unspecified broken thing, which sounds all too much

Sean Gallup, 'People attend a protest rally against racism following the recent death of George Floyd in the USA on May 31, 2020 in Berlin, Germany', 2020

like civility and peace, i.e., the status quo. His decision to deputise the Vietnam War and the shooting of American students at Kent State as precedent could be turned toward a different and more telling analysis though, which is simply this: America, as a nation, is founded in and rests upon forms of legal and extra-legal violence against Black and Brown bodies, native or foreign, at home and abroad. Roughly since lynchings became epidemic in the nineteenth century, as a nation it has borne very partial witness to the ghostly return of its extra-territorial forms of violence back to its own domestic sphere, where they're wielded as practices and technologies of subjugation against American citizens. That's where the practice of lynching originates, and the broader militarisation of policing inside America is an extension of that trajectory. So there's a deep continuum here, not an aberration.

I would agree with Carter that the protest is what's new though. I've been tremendously encouraged to see the role that the still image has played in the waves of protest and resistance in the wake of George Floyd's murder, because they have demonstrated that a new norm has emerged in which the spectacular image of Black death is no longer itself the totem of resistance to anti-Blackness. Instead, this beautiful portrait of George Floyd has become an emblem of the movement, and it's one in which he appears as a fully self-possessed, powerful, thick-lipped, and irreducibly Black man. To me that's tremendously important, and if we think back to the images of Michael Brown circulated immediately following his killing by Darren Wilson, including by the fabled Grey Lady, this marks progress in the realm of the image. It suggests a choice being made along the precise lines of #IfTheyGunnedMeDown.

Denise Ferreira da Silva just contributed a short and intricate piece to a series of short texts by Black feminist thinkers published online by *Canadian Art* magazine under the title 'Thoughts of Liberation', in which she begins: 'Any imaging of otherwise in this world requires contending with the scene, the scene of violence, and with that which captures the when, how and where a Black person was killed by a police officer.'[35]

One might presume that if she is right, and I'd argue that she is – that the route to an *other* world necessarily leads through the natal scene of evisceration – that she's saying we have to dwell in that scene, and replicate it endlessly. But she's not making that claim. I think that I have to spend those nine minutes and twenty-nine seconds in vigil with George Floyd, that I have to suffer that micro-version of his actual death. But da Silva suggests that there is creative work to be done in the wake of that scene, which need not include its reproduction. She argues that that creative work 'must face squarely the ethical-political challenge of working with the visual nowadays, which is to find the balance between visibility and obscurity.' She recognises that 'visualizability – being available via social media and accessible through electronic gadgets – seems to have become the main (if not the sole) criterion for reality', but argues that 'the only way is through these conditions of representation.' I'd agree.

If we think of the massive, bold, yellow, fully capitalised inscriptions of the phrase 'BLACK LIVES MATTER' across the public streets of so many American cities, often in direct and deliberate proximity to buildings that house central elements of American political infrastructure, it's clear that people are continuously seeking a variety of ways of making new images in response to that 'scene', and that these new images – these 'creative works' – don't depend upon a reproduction of the scene of George Floyd's lynching itself. Instead, da Silva argues that the creative move:

> exposes the excess that is the state's use of total violence, of law enforcement as technique of racial subjugation, while simultaneously removing the black person (the father, the sister, the friend) out of the scene of violence and its visualization. It does so by restoring the dimensions of their existence that the camera cannot capture. That is, the creative move must protect (as an ethical gesture) the black person (keeping her obscurity) in the excess that is the very visualization of the scene of total violence.[36]

Shawn M. Pridgen, 'Power to the People - Chi Ossé on the steps of the Brooklyn Public Library main branch', 5 June 2020

This seems apt to me. It brings us back to this concept of the potency of obscurity, or opacity, to use the term in the context in which Édouard Glissant does.[37] It helps me to understand certain aversions I've had about making particular types of images, or of appropriating them, while also feeling a certain compulsion to find a way to images that can visualise, or in some way make palpable some of those structural forces that exceed such terrible scenes. Inscribing the phrase 'BLACK LIVES MATTER' onto the public thoroughfare as a kind of temporary instruction makes visible all the ways that they do not, and opens itself up to that phrase's eventual erasure, which calls for new thinking, new images, new initiatives around how to restore to visibility the state's 'total violence'. The process cannot be static, just as the image also cannot ultimately stand still. This does leave open the door for precisely the risk that you describe, that a kind of meta-commentary in the mainstream press, made up of images about images, can evade or disavow the systemic

Kesh Nthamba, 'Racial Abuse and Police Brutality, Kibra, Kamukunji. A mural depicts George Floyd. In Kenya, thousands have died at the hands of the police. Police brutality has long been a social issue needing attention. Officers guilty of these crimes are never held accountable, introducing yet another grave concern of the impunity lurking deep in Kenya's judicial system', 3 June 2020

forces that these new images bring into visibility. But we can't swear off the responsibility to fight in that realm, or at least that's what I think. What about you?

DC: I'm inclined to feel, along with Denise Ferreira da Silva, that what is salutary is the understanding that at the level of the image, political response is creative response. There does seem to be a quite widespread realisation of this, and the consequence is a widening out of visual strategies beyond the iconic and totemic uses of particular images. Nobody knows which visual strategies really work, and none will work everywhere, for everyone, so there's a will to experiment rather than cling to any particular mode of visualisation or address. Language – slogans, questions, demands, debate – is extremely effective, and at least it has the advantage of not deriving so directly from particulars the way that photographic images inevitably do. Moreover, language itself can be imaged. The giant 'BLACK LIVES MATTER' lettering on so many streets is not only on those streets: it's in the images made of those streets. And think of all the social media images of written placards and posters, for example. Articulate and pointed, they sidestep the reifying and co-optable silence of the still image. Photography is being understood and embraced as the scripto-visual hybrid it always was, and for emergent and urgent ends. Images, in the pure sense, cannot do it all. I think the anxiety that many feel about the contemporary image regime is that it does seem to put itself forward as if it *can* do it all, and that one must accept visibility on its terms. Images are woefully lacking in so many ways, particularly still and mute images. The picturing of text is an important response to this shortcoming. The media theorist in me suspects that one of the pre-conditions for the widespread emergence of text-as-image is the rebus-like nature of social media, with its fluid interchange between images, words, images of words, symbols, emojis, and so forth. Interestingly, this kind of hybridity is closer to the structure of the unconscious, which makes no hard distinction between word and image. (This requires a lot of unpacking, I know, but I feel it is worth mentioning in this context).

But to your broader point, there is a lot at stake as to what the 'realm' of the image and the fight over the image really are, and how they are constituted. Are the terms fixed and given in advance, along the lines of Jacques Rancière's 'consensual categories' of the media that are somehow always already capable of withstanding and absorbing calls for change, like a pressure valve, in such a way that they facilitate the return to the neoliberal status quo? Or is the realm more radically open and capable of being kept open? This is not a new question, and perhaps rather than formulating an answer it might be a question that has to be asked constantly and vigilantly, theoretically and practically.

22 Mark Fisher, 'The Metaphysics of Crackle: Afrofuturism and Hauntology', *Dancecult: Journal of Electronic Dance Music Culture*, 5:2 (2013), p. 48.

23 Sheldon George, *Trauma and Race: A Lacanian Study of African American Racial Identity* (Waco: Baylor University Press, 2016).

24 Paul Gilroy and Ruth Wilson Gilmore (eds), *Stuart Hall: Selected Writings on Race and Difference* (Durham NC, Duke University Press, 2021).

25 Abigail Solomon-Godeau, 'Who Is Speaking Thus? Some Questions about Documentary Photography', *Photography at the Dock: Essays on Photographic History, Institutions, and Practices* (Minneapolis: University of Minnesota Press, 1994).

26 Elizabeth Alexander, 'The Trayvon Generation', *The New Yorker*, 15 June 2020 <https://www.newyorker.com/magazine/2020/06/22/the-trayvon-generation>

27 Kendrick Lamar, 'Alright' (2015), directed by Colin Tilley <https://www.youtube.com/watch?v=Z-48u_uWMHY>

28 Flying Lotus, 'Until the Quiet Comes' (2012), directed by Kahlil Joseph, featuring Storyboard P <https://vimeo.com/48551671>

29 Mike Baker, Jennifer Valentino-DeVries, Manny Fernandez, and Michael LaForgia, 'Three Words. 70 Cases. The Tragic History of "I Can't Breathe."', *The New York Times*, 29 June 2020 <https://www.nytimes.com/interactive/2020/06/28/us/i-cant-breathe-police-arrest.html>

30 Roland Barthes, 'The Third Meaning', *Image Music Text* trans. by Stephen Heath (London: Fontana Press, 1977), pp. 52–68.

31 Rabih Mroué, *The Pixelated Revolution* (2012), excerpted at <https://vimeo.com/119433287>

32 'Scenes for a New Heritage: Contemporary Art from the Collection', Museum of Modern Art, NY, 15 March 2015 – 11 April 2016, curated by Quentin Bajac, Eva Respini, Ana Janevski, and Sarah Suzuki.

33 Maurice Blanchot, 'The Two Versions of the Imaginary', *The Space of Literature* trans. by Ann Smock (Lincoln: University of Nebraska Press, 1982), pp. 254–263.

34 Graydon Carter, 'George Floyd's killing and how an image can change history', *GQ*, 9 June 2020 <https://www.gq-magazine.co.uk/news/article/george-floyd-image>

35 Denise Ferreira da Silva, 'Thoughts of Liberation', *Canadian Art Journal*, 17 June 2020 <https://canadianart.ca/features/thoughts-of-liberation/>

36 Ibid.

37 'If we examine the process of 'understanding' people and ideas from the perspective of Western thought, we discover that its basis is this requirement for transparency. In

order to understand and thus accept you, I have to measure your solidity with the ideal scale providing me with grounds to make comparisons and, perhaps, judgments. I have to reduce. [...] I understand your difference, or in other words, without creating a hierarchy, I relate it to my norm. I admit you to existence, within my system. I create you afresh—But perhaps we need to bring an end to the very notion of a scale. Displace all reduction. Agree not merely to the right to difference but, carrying this further, agree also to the right to opacity that is not enclosure within an impenetrable autarchy but subsistence within an irreducible singularity. Opacities can coexist and converge, weaving fabrics. To understand these truly one must focus on the texture of the weave and not on the nature of its components. For the time being, perhaps, give up this old obsession with discovering what lies at the bottom of natures. There would be something great and noble about initiating such a movement, referring not to Humanity but to the exultant divergence of humanities.' Édouard Glissant, 'For Opacity', *Poetics of Relation* (Ann Arbor: The University of Michigan Press, 1997). pp. 189–190.

PART TWO

The itinerant image

Stanley Wolukau-Wanambwa: Let's turn to the complex relations of photography to time: time as expressed by the image itself; the relation of the image to its historical moment; and the afterlife of the image as it passes through time. These relations inform many of your own writings and curatorial projects. Your book and exhibition *a Handful of Dust* (2015) retrace a history of photographic modernism and the transformation of modern life from roughly 1920 to 2015, and they do so by way of a photograph that eventually came to be known as *Dust Breeding*. The photograph depicts (although it doesn't necessarily suggest) the receptive surface of a piece of glass upon which dust has been steadily gathering, and it somehow condenses into a single image photography's tendency to record, reflect, resemble, dissemble, and receive. I think it's an especially apt motif to use for the journey you set out on. How did you arrive at this point of departure?

David Campany: Looking at the interplay of the temporalities within photographs and around them can be very illuminating and instructive. Aesthetically, culturally, politically. It's that combination of the ontological and the social: attending to the specifics of the image and the medium, while also thinking through the cultural and historical situations in which the image finds itself, or in which it is put to work. I think this approach recurs in my work because it was there at the beginning for me. My first visual fascination was with film stills, which have such complicated relations to time and context. And then as soon as photography became an interest I began to notice the same images coming up in different settings. Images get re-used, and whatever temporal qualities they may have are framed by cultural contexts.

I first saw *Dust Breeding* back in 1989, as an undergraduate student. It was in an exhibition at London's Royal Academy, celebrating 150 years of photography. I thought it looked so strange and ugly. I remember not liking it at all, and it didn't seem to fit with anything. It bore no relation to anything, or at least it struck me that way at the time. It was made in 1920 just before the onset of surrealism and the New Vision but it doesn't look like it belongs to either. I was intrigued that

Man Ray, *Dust Breeding*, 1920, from *a Handful of Dust* (2015)

two artists had signed it: Man Ray and Marcel Duchamp. The dust is gathering on Duchamp's great artwork *The Bride Stripped Bare by her Bachelors, Even* (aka the *Large Glass*, 1915–1923), which was then still unfinished. Scratching around for information, I noted that in books on Man Ray the photograph was often presented as a visionary work of art. But in Duchamp books, it was more of a document or anecdote of the making of the *Large Glass*.

Three years later I was working in an arts bookshop in London when Sophie Ristelhueber published *Fait*, her book of photographs of the Kuwaiti desert, taken shortly after the invading Iraqi army had retreated. In an interview, Ristelhueber cited *Dust Breeding*, with its ambiguous sense of scale and place, as the visual template for her own project. It seemed so intriguing to me that a photograph that was then seventy years of age had that kind of hold on a photographer, and

Sophie Ristelhueber, *Because of The Dust Breeding*, 1991–2007, from *a Handful of Dust* (2015)

that kind of relevance to a completely different artistic and political context.

From then on *Dust Breeding* was firmly in my consciousness and I started to notice more affiliations, associations, resonances, and influences. You can see that image as a precursor to the early work of Bruce Nauman, for example. The first major survey show of conceptual art, *Information* (1970) at the Museum of Modern Art, New York, included *Dust Breeding* as a keynote image for the art to come. Rosalind Krauss wrote about it in her landmark essay 'Notes on the Index', 1977.[38] Many contemporary artists are still drawn to it. In 2006, I was asked by Sophie Howarth to write an essay on a photograph of my choice, for a book titled *Singular Images*.[39] I chose *Dust Breeding* and with that short text I realised there was so much more to explore. The relation between entropy, destruction, and creativity. Traces and ruins as political allegories. The always hybrid and elusive status of the photographic image, regardless of the claims made on its behalf.

Beyond all that, I had interests in the challenge of how to resolve a complex set of ideas as both a book and an exhibition. How to address the specificity of each, so that the exhibition doesn't feel like it ought to be a book, and vice versa, which can happen with highly 'researched' projects, ending up like theses on the wall. And in this instance I realised the key to it was to try and make it feel like a sort of high-wire act (I didn't have to try that hard because for me it really was a high wire act). The project became a speculation about the affinities and often subconscious connections we make between images. How does one do that in a way that might feel really generative and even emancipatory for a reader/viewer, rather than indulgent on the part of the author/curator?

SW-W: There's something in that history of *Dust Breeding's* evolving affinities to other artists and critics over time that clarifies photography's extraordinarily adaptive nature. You write in the book that 'photography is unmoored and porous, belonging everywhere and nowhere, right across modern culture, and not just to art'.[40] Photography has been the willing servant of such radically distinct masters over time. How did you set about tracing a path in images 'from the cosmic to the domestic', as you subtitle your long essay in the book, and how did you think through ways of dealing with photography's mobility?

DC: In his 1963 memoir, *Self Portrait*, Man Ray describes how the dust photograph came about. He had been asked to document works in the collection of Katherine S. Dreier, who was then setting up the Société Anonyme (a sort of forerunner to the Museum of Modern Art) and she needed images for press and publicity. Man Ray recalled: 'The thought of photographing the work of others was repugnant to me, beneath my dignity as an artist'.[41] But he needed the money, and copy-work was becoming a way for photographers to ingratiate themselves with art folk, and get paid too. At Duchamp's studio he was grumbling about this request, and Duchamp suggested he practice with the dusty sheet of glass.

I have always been interested in the idea of copy-work being the basis, or even *baseness*, of photography, and that a photographer with artistic ambition might be made anxious by it. It is an idea that really haunts all of photography, but it energises it too. Whatever the artistic ambitions, there remains a degree of plain, automated copying in all photography. One of my aims here was to trace the arc of that anxiety and possibility, and to do it through the substance and metaphor of dust, something very base indeed. I think automated copying and dust are linked in photography. Dust is usually what you get as a side effect, both in modern life and in photography. There's an unlikely kinship there. I can formulate it quite clearly now, but for a long while I was intuiting this and following my nose to a whole range of photographic practices and works from across the last century. These then got reconsidered much more soberly, and over time they were whittled down to a group or lineage that made some kind of sense to me. It included everything from postcards and press photos of dust storms to avant-garde journal articles, conceptual art works, surrealist photography, and documentary photography. The mobility you mention, of photography's multiple places and uses and slippages, was something I felt could be alluded to by a careful selection and sequence of the images that interested me, without much recourse to words. Across pages, around walls.

Selecting and sequencing images: over the years this has become my approach to writing. Images first, then words. The 'image track' of the book of *a Handful of Dust* presents all the works one to a page or spread, around 150 of them, arranged to articulate various affinities. Then there's an insert with a long essay, which includes the works reproduced as small thumbnail illustrations. A viewer/reader can approach it image-to-image, wordlessly, or more theoretically through my writing. Hopefully they'll do both, feeling the differences and similarities. But I'm pleased that we found a form for the book that kept them apart.

38   Rosalind Krauss, 'Notes on the Index', *OCTOBER*, 3 (Spring 1977), pp. 68–81.
39   Sophie Howarth (ed.), *Singular Images: Essays on Remarkable Photographs* (London: Tate, 2006).
40   David Campany, *a Handful of Dust* (London: MACK, 2015), p. 13.
41   Man Ray, *Self Portrait* (London: André. Deutsch Limited, 1963), pp. 78–80.

Blurred lines

SW-W: There's a nice echo there of the visual grammar of Walker Evans's book *American Photographs* (1938), and also of Volker Kahmen's *Art History of Photography* (1974). That method of arraying the images certainly helps to clarify visual and conceptual affinities between works we might not typically 'think' together, like Alfred Stieglitz's photograph of Marcel Duchamp's *Fountain* and Paul Strand's *Photograph – New York* (later titled *Blind Woman*). How did you approach installing the works in the show at Le Bal?

DC: Yes, it's a *complementary* relation between text and image, rather than a supplementary relation of text *to* image: the two not quite servicing each other, not quite in harmony, but playing off each other.

Le Bal has two rooms. The smaller upper room had a vitrine containing every major appearance in print of the Man Ray/Duchamp image, from its first publication in 1922, in the avant-garde journal *Littérature*, where it was described as a 'view from an aeroplane', to its use in the MoMA catalogue for the 1970 exhibition 'Information', via various publications such as *Minotaure* and *View*. Around the walls there would be all manner of things, from aerial reconnaissance photos to works by photographers such as Wols

Martin Argyroglo, installation views of 'a Handful of Dust: from the Cosmic to the Domestic', Le Bal, Paris (2015–16)

who used impoverished and marginal materials. There were press photos and postcards of dust storms, images of the nuclear destruction of Hiroshima and Nagasaki, and more. So a weave of major and minor themes, catastrophes and the everyday, major events and impressions of almost nothing.

The downstairs space is very big. Here I placed post-1960s work. Bruce Nauman, playing with flour on his studio floor. Robert Filliou, cleaning paintings in the Louvre and preserving his dusty cloths along with Polaroids of his activity. John Divola's *Vandalism* (1974–75), a suite of photographs taken in deserted homes where he becomes a sort of arty vandal, creating as he destroys and documenting his activities. We come up to date with more explicitly political works, such as Sophie Ristelhueber's *Fait*, and projects by Xavier Ribas, Louise Oates, Eva Stenram, and Gerhard Richter, and images by Robert Burley, Rut Blees Luxemburg, Jeff Wall, and others. As with the book, the show invites the viewer to make connections, but without offering any explicit 'script for looking'.

I think there was a feeling of surprise for audiences that a project involving such unlikely and abject images could be engaging. *a Handful of Dust* dodges so many of the expectations of contemporary art and photography. There are almost no images of people, few recognisable places, very few obvious signs of artistic authorship, few seductive colours, little one might think of as 'beautiful', and the presentation is quite sombre. There are a lot of themes held together gently. Moreover, the intent is quite different to the tendency in exhibitions and books to convey a clear 'message' or thesis. A project can be engaging and thoughtful and well-researched but still feel provisional and respectful of what a reader/viewer might bring to it. Of course, that is risky. It can fall very flat. There is no formula. No set path. But these are strange times, and I sense there is an understanding that they call for strange responses. Even when a book or show 'doesn't work', what matters is *how* it doesn't work. Better an original failure than an unoriginal success.

There is a politics in this, of course, but it is inchoate and somewhat unpredictable, since it is not about direct and agreed communication but the encouraging of response. It's what John Cage called 'response-ability': the responsibility to respond, on terms that are not given in advance, but discovered and invented in the midst of things.

SW-W: You've talked before about photography's moment of ascendancy in visual culture at the height of the picture press, and your interests, books, and exhibitions encompass a broader church of photographic uses and users than the traditional art historical canon.[42] Many of the works deal with tumultuous events (like war, famine, and death), or propose a shift in conventionally stable cultural categories (like Walker Evans's magazine piece 'Color Accidents', made for *Architectural Forum* magazine in 1958). This reminds me of Allan Sekula's claim in 'The Body and the Archive' that 'photography is modernity run riot', which I think encapsulates both the transformative effect of technology and the industrial revolution and the way the camera itself changes practices in utterly unrelated non-art fields (like criminology).[43] How did you think about change and transformation in your projects?

DC: Sekula was right, I think. To follow photography really *is* to follow it running riot, in and as modernity. It scrambled the cultural hierarchy that put museums and canons at the top, books lower down, magazines still further, and websites grubbing along the bottom. It's been interesting to see museums respond to this, becoming places that might incorporate all the outlets and platforms that are created, adapted, or adopted by photography. Museums may still be platforms in their own right, but they have also become places simply

Walker Evans, 'Color Accidents', *Architectural Forum,* January 1958

to look again at all the other platforms, past and present. So I have no problem putting a magazine spread in proximity to a Jeff Wall photograph, or a once discarded press photo or postcard alongside a consecrated masterwork by Edward Weston or Laure Albin-Guillot. Sure, it presents its own challenges and pitfalls, and one has to be on one's toes, both as a curator and a viewer, but that's all to the good. I can't imagine it any other way. Plus of course, images in the mind know no barriers. There they mix and inform each other. I feel we should accept this and work with it. In many ways the running riot is a running away from authorship as the key to meaning, and towards contexts, discourses, institutions, and viewers as being much more determinant. Again, there's a politics to this that by its nature must not be overprescribed. A politics of possibility.

42   David Campany, 'Photography, Encore' in *Time Present: Photography from the Deutsche Bank Collection* (Frankfurt: Deutsche Bank AG, 2014), pp. 22–33.
43   Sekula, 'The Body and the Archive', p. 101.

Margin as foundation

SW-W: The photographs that bookend the sequence of plates in your book appear to be non-art images that recall to an art audience the work of Stan Douglas and Christopher Williams, specifically in their practice of reframing quotidian photographic forms and rhetorics. In this book, and your two previous ones (*The Open Road: Photography and the American Roadtrip* (2014) and *Walker Evans: The Magazine Work* (2014)) you have insisted on the co-equal status of non-art photographic images to understanding the medium, in recognition of photographic art's irreducible links to popular culture and public space.

DC: It's interesting that photography became important to contemporary art by becoming a kind of operating table, a place for taking apart or remaking its non-art practices. Think of modernist art photography in the 'documentary style', or later the artist as archivist, the artist as still life photographer, the artist in the guise of the news photographer, the artist as industrial photographer, the artist as fashion photographer, the artist as guileless snapshot photographer, and so on. That was inevitable and has produced at least some extraordinary work. Speaking personally however, I've never felt I needed art or an artist to help me 'see' the

Photographer unknown, 'ACME Agency School children blow 26 days of dust from their books as striking teachers return to work', 23 March 1948, from *a Handful of Dust* (2015)

common vernacular practices for what they are, in all their complexity. They are just as interesting on their own terms. So, for example, I find the artist Stan Douglas's reimaginings of a postwar press photographer (his series *Midcentury Studio*, 2011) no more or less engaging or significant than the work of postwar press photographers themselves. I suspect Douglas does too. I am just as stimulated looking at cold war-era commercial studio photography on eBay or in vintage books as I am contemplating Christopher Williams' arch ventriloquism of it in prestigious museums. And I suspect he is too. I remember as an undergraduate student seeing images by Cindy Sherman from her series *Untitled Film Stills* (1977–80). I thought they were absolutely fascinating, and still do. But since I was a kid I had been collecting discarded film publicity stills, shot by working photographers whose names are long lost, and these were just as compelling to me. Narrative allusion; the distillation and estrangement of cinematic desire and spectatorship; the slippages between acting and posing. The 'art photographer as guide to vernacular photography' is a very interesting position, and it has a rich history going all the way back to the 1920s at least. Even so, I don't need my hand held in that way, and I like to suggest to readers of my books, and visitors to exhibitions that I put together, that they don't need their hand held either.

SW-W: That reminds me of Siegfried Kracauer's argument in 'The Anteroom' that the photographic media:

> help us to think through things, not above them. Otherwise expressed, the photographic media make it much easier for us to incorporate the transient phenomena of the outer world, thereby redeeming them from oblivion.[44]

So much of the work in *a Handful of Dust* directs our attention toward the at once eloquent and recalcitrant matter of the earth: Xavier Ribas's fantastic series *Nomads* (2008) for instance, or Lewis Baltz's *Nevada* (1977) to name just a couple. You talk in the essay about photographs 'turning background into foreground, ground into figure'.[45] How do you account for photography's fascination with the vagaries and textures of the ground on which we walk, and its influence on other art practices?

DC: I think that comes with any lens-based image: it takes in the world whole, all at once, the desired stuff and the undesired stuff. It has a radical sense of contingency that always threatens to give intention the slip, and to tip the image into chaos or chance. For photographers this is often a problem, until they learn to handle it. Baltz and Ribas have been very elemental about it, whereas a photographer like Lee Friedlander accepts the chaos, delicately marshalling it into a picture that can then contemplate it.

Many of the earliest commentators on photography noticed its capacity to pick up all manner of little details without the 'author' having to fuss over their presence. Think of Fox Talbot in *The Pencil of Nature* (1844–46) noting how photography incorporates levels of visual information that only the most pedantic painter would see fit to include. Moreover, that very background condition often underpins the 'reality effect' of photography, to borrow Roland Barthes's literary phrase. The nondescript, undesired extras we get in a picture actually have a vital role. This is why if you Photoshop all the unwanted stuff out of a photograph, it ends up not looking like a photograph. Well, what would a picture be if it were comprised entirely of the stuff we don't usually want? What if the background was the foreground? What if the secondary stuff was primary? That's one way of understanding *Dust Breeding*: an image that turns photography's marginalia into its very reason for being. But actually that dynamic is present in any photographic image to some extent. To your point though, I have long been interested in the difference between moving through the world with one's head up and moving through it with one's head down. One can think of interwar modernist photography in those terms. Those that point the camera up, and those that point it down. I'm simplifying, of course, but someone should compile a book just of interwar photographs of that gutter space where the sidewalk meets the road. Kertész. Wols. Bing. Krull. Brassaï. Lotar. Evans. So many. I think in such images there is a 'lyric of the streets' and an understanding that, as Walter Benjamin put it, in modernity every street is the scene of a crime.

I like what you say about the matter of the earth. I think it really is eloquent and recalcitrant, and the two are deeply connected. This is what allows *a Handful of Dust* to sketch a path between poetry and violence, for example. There are very few images of human bodies in the project, and when they do appear they are quite intense carriers of both. For example, in the exhibition I include a couple of minutes of the prologue of Alain Resnais's 1959 film *Hiroshima, Mon Amour*, a love story scripted by Marguerite Duras about a Japanese survivor of nuclear holocaust and a French survivor of the horrors of the war in Europe. Resnais films their bodies intimately, the sweat on their skin slowly becoming covered in dust. The mere presence of the word 'Hiroshima' signals the possibility that this dust is nuclear. In voice-over a man states flatly: 'You saw nothing in Hiroshima'. Immediately the status of vision, visibility and evidence are in question, suspended so that they become openly thinkable and not taken for granted. In many ways I consider *a Handful of Dust* a deeply bodily and embodied project, even though this may not be the immediate impression. I tend to come at the poetic and the violent obliquely. Of course, all violence, and all poetic affect is located at the level of the body, but I find it is often more productive to approach the question indirectly.

SW-W: The absorbent characteristics of photography play a crucial role here. You've talked about photography's complex relation to texture and to its surface, which Craigie Horsfield calls 'the place of its evasion'.[46] One could argue that the piece of the *Large Glass* photographed in *Dust Breeding* embodies the accretion of matter over time on a physical surface, but the photograph *Dust Breeding* symbolises the way that reproducibility 'chases away' surface in a photographic image. I'm interested in your assertion in the book's essay that 'photography gives up the textural for the textual, so to speak. It triumphs through a suppression of its material surface and an implicit acceptance that its modernity is connected to the printed page and knowledge.'[47] Can you expand on that?

DC: One could think about this through a well-rehearsed if slightly caricatured moment in the emergence of photographic modernism, in which it ceases to fight its own industrial basis and instead embraces it. Late pictorialist photography, with its fussy hand-brushed emulsions and forced cultivation of a photographic surface, gives way to a smooth industrial surface, but in so doing, it opens up the medium's capacity to describe the surfaces of the world. Think of how modernist photography, let's say between the 1920s and the 1950s, was so preoccupied with texture. 'Polished steel and palpitating flesh' was an expression used by Edward Weston.[48] But in a wider sense, photography could report back on the surfaces around it and contribute to knowledge or appreciation of the world only if it surrendered the interferences of its own surface – only if it 'evaded' it, to use Horsfield's phrase.

SW-W: You talk then about the kind of synchronised inverse relationship to surface occurring around the mid-century between photography's modernist drive toward a transparent surface and abstract expressionist painting's move toward a reflexive obsession with its non-representational surface. It's interesting to note the extent to which a lot of contemporary fine art photography now directs our attention reflexively back toward the digital substrate of modern images, and to the illusionistic relationship photographs establish to the material world. The dust now is the pixel in the screen rather than the mote hanging in the air.

DC: I've long been interested in modern photography's acceptance of its elusive industrial smoothness occurring at exactly the same time painting was becoming modern by foregrounding its own. There's so much at stake in this I feel it deserves its own book – and I'm not sure I'm the one to write it. But I can't help thinking that art photography's current thrashing about in an attempt to articulate some sense of surface is another iteration of its long-standing ambivalence about its essential surfacelessness. 'Essential' in the sense that an image formed by light has no materiality, and the substrate is always secondary, deriving from the attempt to make it manifest as an object.

SW-W: It's funny that you describe the conflict in those terms, because when Richard Learoyd gave a talk at Aperture about his first comprehensive monograph, he said that the image refracted into his camera obscura is the most perfect one, and that the fixed photograph (or any fixed photograph) is a degradation of that almost platonic original.[49]

DC: That's interesting. I think I agree. In general (although there are exceptions), in photography there is 'capture' and then there is 'output'. It's a procedure very different to painting, for example. Arguably a photographic image has no intrinsic scale or materiality or surface. Those are secondary choices. And while a viewer may not think about this consciously, I would guess they intuit it. To look at a photograph on a wall is to look at a choice that has been made. And innumerable choices were possible. Many things can be done with the same image capture, and while some of those things may be more appropriate than others, or more interesting, or more thoughtful, all are on some level legitimate possibilities.

This also means that photographs have an uncanny, chameleon-like relation to contexts. When one sees a photograph reproduced on a page, for example, one rarely thinks it is out of place, or that it belongs somewhere else. It seems to belong wherever it appears, while at the same time looking provisional, because it could equally belong elsewhere too. That is the genius and the curse of photography, I suspect, and one of the preconditions of its modern 'running riot'. It's important that as writers, curators, and image-makers we think carefully about this. Such indeterminacy shapes so much of our culture and not all for the bad, by any means. I'm thinking about how some contemporary photographic artists resolve their projects in parallel ways, as both books and exhibitions at the same time, for example. Meanwhile others might conceive their projects solely in terms of the specificities of just one context. A book *or* an exhibition. More broadly though, we'd have to accept that contemporary visual culture is dominated by the generally promiscuous and only sometimes strategic circulation of immaterial images online. The forces that shape such circulation – algorithms, the rise and fall of social issues, trends, zeitgeists. This is the background and foreground.

44 Siegfried Kracauer, 'The Anteroom', *History: The Last Things Before the Last* (Princeton: Markus Wiener Publishers, 1995), p. 192.

45 Campany, *a Handful of Dust*, p. 25.

46 Craigie Horsfield, '30th August 1992, Rotterdam', in *Im Gespräch/Conversation* (Köln: DuMont, 1999), p. 184.

47 Campany, *a Handful of Dust*, p. 35.

48 Edward Weston, entry for 10 March 1924 in *The Daybooks of Edward Weston* (New York: Aperture, 1973), quoted in Nancy Newhall (ed.), *Edward Weston: the flame of Recognition* (London: Gordon Fraser, 1975), p.12.

49 Richard Learoyd In Conversation with Chris McCall, *Aperture In Person*, 28 October 2015, Aperture Gallery and Bookstore, New York, NY.

PART THREE

A question of time(liness)

David Campany: On the subject of indeterminacy, I'm struck by the fact that your book *One Wall a Web* doesn't 'add up'. By which I mean it does not offer a single position, a single attitude to images or writing that would permit the book to cohere easily. It's an *uneasy* work. It doesn't deliver a message or signal a particularly clear attitude, even though the last text is more emphatic. How did you and your publisher come to a sense that it was ready for publication, and finished, or 'definitively unfinished', to use that great Marcel Duchamp expression?

Stanley Wolukau-Wanambwa: I was very interested in the possibility of making a book that *kept happening to you* from the front cover all the way to the back cover, and in that sense I was invested in a method that kept opening things up wider and wider over time. I think that we knew it was definitively unfinished at a point where our revisions made fractional differences to the good and more often made things worse.

DC: I agree that books must take their own time, in the making and in the viewing. Moreover, I find the temporality of books to be very complicated. Books are not disposed of, at least not in the way other kinds of printed matter such as magazines are. Consciously or unconsciously, to make a book is to think about posterity, or at least to accept an unspecified cultural moment to come. But a peculiar dynamic has developed around photographic books in the last decade or so, which puts the emphasis of reception firmly on the now, on the present. There's an expectation that books be timely, deal with issues of the moment, and be comprehensible to the present. It's a strange burden of expectation to place on a book, this form that must take its own time to arrive and its own time to find an audience. There are plenty of other forms and platforms that are more immediate. What do you feel about the life and temporality of books?

SW-W: I'm a big fan of the work of the Chilean filmmaker Patricio Guzmán, and I've been re-watching his trilogy of recent films (*Nostalgia for the Light* (2010); *The Pearl Button* (2015); *The Cordillera of Dreams* (2019)) quite a lot this past year. He fled Chile not too long after the US-backed coup that put Pinochet into power, having made an extraordinary and justly canonical documentary in three parts about that period called *La Batalla de Chile* (1975–79). All his work has been about Chile, though the vast majority has been made while he has lived in exile or abroad.

In the recent trilogy, he takes three forms of matter – light, water, and mountains – and by extension three phenomena that shape the geography and geology of Chile as lenses through which to contend with the nation's history. The films examine the struggles of those who have lived in the shadows of Chile's planned amnesia, and in opposition to it, and sets those experiences in the context of larger questions about astronomical and geological time, settler colonial violence and political repression.

One of the central assertions, or insights of the first film is that we all live in the past. Guzmán speaks with an astrophysicist who works in an observatory in the Atacama Desert, where there's no humidity, and thus where far-seeing into the universe is most easily practised, and they explain that we all experience the world at a certain delay from the instant itself. The noise of this keyboard takes a millionth of a second to travel from the keypad to my ear, your voice is fractionally delayed as it reaches me on the phone, the light reflecting off the apartment building opposite the window in front of me takes some fractional instants to arrive. The argument of the astrophysicist is that the present, as such, does not exist – that we weave it out of a tapestry of delay.

I say this not just to agree that seeing what it is that defines 'the' moment is extraordinarily hard, and tremendously unlikely in the instant of its occurrence, but also because I think that that's how I've approached image-making, not just in *One Wall a Web*, and certainly not solely in the guise of the appropriated archival negatives in *All My Gone Life*, but really in all the kinds of forms of seeing I practise. I've tried to reckon with making images as an exercise in which one can be in productive dialogue with multiple temporalities that coalesce and diverge at varying levels of perceptibility in the world at all times. Constantly.

To say that is not to try to relativise the role that certain fundamental realities we might describe as 'timely', to use your word, play in the work, but rather to say that those realities are also inherently historical and multifold, that they're entangled in a much thicker and broader weave, and that there are, or hopefully there can be, many ways to engage with what the work makes visible – the preponderance of which I'll never be able to anticipate, because the book will outlive me. And so yes, I also definitely made the book with a thought to that unassimilable future toward which it's moving, and in which it might play a wide variety of roles.

Stanley Wolukau-Wanambwa, *Hermitage Rd*, 2014, from the series *All My Gone Life* (2014–16)

Stanley Wolukau-Wanambwa, *S. Sycamore Street*, 2014, from the series *All My Gone Life* (2014–16)

You and I are in dialogue less than a handful of days after an attempted coup was staged in the US Capitol on 6 January, in which armed white supremacists set out not merely to impede or reverse the certification of the results of a national election, but also to do lethal violence to the elected officials who would participate in that process. They brought Molotov cocktails, pipe bombs, high-capacity magazines for semi-automatic rifles, zip ties, a guillotine, a noose, handguns and bullets, and they did this not merely in Washington, DC, but at state capitols across the nation. The results they wanted to decertify were the aggregate choice of preponderantly Black and Brown voters in Detroit, Philadelphia, Pittsburgh, Atlanta, Las Vegas, and Phoenix – votes that swung the electoral college comprehensively to the Biden column.

In his 1985 essay *The Evidence of Things Not Seen*, James Baldwin observes that for Black people, '*ancestral* and *daily* are synonyms', which brings us back to Guzmán, and also to a question about who is able to live in the world as though it had no history and who is not.[50] The white riot has an electoral history in the United States, by which I mean it has productively (re)shaped the conditions of political agency in this nation, as we have been reminded these past few days. Those of us who warned in 2016 that armed insurrectionist white nationalists would leap to the defence of Trump should he be voted out were dismissed as fantasists in that moment. Even now, as it continues to happen, in Kentucky, Washington state, and elsewhere, still there is a denial that the weight of that history shapes the conditions in which Black and Brown people struggle to make life in the US. Baldwin writes:

It is absolutely impossible for Authority or bureaucracy to scent danger as swiftly as does the menaced human being. Authority can scent danger only to itself. It demands a crisis of whatever proportions before the private danger can be perceived as menacing the public safety.[51]

I'd argue that we've been able to hear Baldwin now – and recently – as a consequence of the reality of the claim that those astrophysicists make: because we live in the past, and our present is made up of its delayed effects.

DC: And those delays come with different intensities which require and challenge our vigilance. Baldwin's observations on how the menaced individual will sense the dangerous antagonisms of an unresolved past remind me of Walter Benjamin in the sixth of his 'Theses on the Philosophy of History':

To articulate the past historically does not mean to recognize it 'the way it really was' (Ranke). It means to seize hold of a memory as it flashes up at a moment of danger. Historical materialism wishes to retain that image of the past which unexpectedly appears to man singled out by history at a moment of danger. The danger affects both the content of the tradition and its receivers. The same threat hangs over both: that of becoming a tool of the ruling classes. In every era the attempt must be made anew to wrest tradition away from a conformism that is about to overpower it.[52]

Benjamin was writing in 1940, in Vichy France, just before his doomed attempt to flee to Spain and beyond, in the midst of catastrophe, and the text itself is subject to deferred reception. Baldwin seems to be read today with greater intensity than ever, and with the recognition that the situations he was describing and diagnosing are still with us. 'Delayed effects', as you put it.

Clearly, a book – carefully worked out, designed, sequenced, bound – now constitutes an emphatically slow form, but also a fixed form that is less subject to the mangling and fragmentation that typifies the online fate of photographic projects. That's part of the appeal of books to makers and audiences today, I imagine. A book may allow greater complexity and nuance than an exhibition ordinarily permits, particularly for image/text work. The risk, of course, is that the book form is becoming quite specialised. I was thinking recently about experimental books from the past. Roy DeCarava and Langston Hughes's *The Sweet Flypaper of Life* (1955) had a print run of 25,000 (22,000 in the cheap but well-produced paperback, 3,000 in hardcover). Initially there were 17,000 copies of Susan Meiselas's *Nicaragua* (1981), bought by people interested in what was going on there and in Central America more widely. When *Nicaragua* was republished it was more of a 'Susan Meiselas' book and for a much smaller audience. But then Walker Evans and James Agee's *Let Us Now Praise Famous Men* – photographs and words rejected by *Fortune* magazine in 1936, published as a book in 1941 – sold just 199 copies in its first two years, and was remaindered at 19 cents a copy. 750 copies were sold at a loss, although it eventually sold out its print run of 1,025 copies. It is not until its 'moment' is seemingly long past that their book reaches a substantial audience. In 1960 it was reprinted, and heralded as a work 'ahead of its time'. But it barely had the chance to be *of* its time. Perhaps it could never have been, for various reasons. We still have very little idea as to exactly how books are engaged with, at a forensic, granular level. This is something that is almost impossible to assess.

Your text at the end of *One Wall a Web* is a thinking through of Blackness and Black subjectivity, often with metaphors that might pertain to photography. Light, darkness, voids, inversions, shadows, traps, fixings, blindnesses, infinities. It's not a text that addresses the photographic medium as such, ontologically, but it certainly strikes me as a theoretical and autobiographical reflection informed by your involvement with photography. You began by noting the impact on your thinking of Black studies. I meant to ask: does that engagement correspond with you being in the US? Does it revolve around aspects of Black studies that are specific to the US?

SW-W: Yes, absolutely, and it seemed very quickly like a matter of psychic survival that I try to close the gap I felt as a Black man raised in a country (the United Kingdom) with no such institutional and academic form as 'African American Studies', who suddenly found himself living in the capital of the confederacy. I think I gravitated toward Black studies for various reasons, some intellectual but others intuitive. I spent quite a bit of time working in neighbourhoods that were majority Black making photographs through graduate school, and I just kept having to ask myself: 'how have Black people survived here?' It seemed (and still seems) so utterly implausible. Gradually those questions opened out in linked ways to a wider reckoning with the generative role of white supremacy, and the fraught and irreconcilable forms of violence it metes out through racial difference along a whole spectrum. It was only a few weeks after I arrived in the US that 'we' learned the full circumstances surrounding Trayvon Martin's murder, and then of course Adam Lanza butchered twenty schoolchildren, and the question of the histories of such violence became quite urgent for me.

I was reading Fred Moten's remarkable essay 'Black Mo'nin'' around that time, and in it his reading of Nathaniel Mackey, and I was slowly beginning to think of different modes of being that are on the one hand enforced by the constitutive violences of white supremacy but on the other create fugitive conditions for evading it, or that have occasioned other desires, ideas, and ways of being in the world.[53] It occurred to me that there is that homology between the strange temporality of the photograph's being in the world and the estranged relationship to presence (and to 'the present') that racial difference imposes upon Black bodies under white supremacy. Even though he wouldn't have known it, Roland Barthes describes something of the classic moment of epidermalisation recounted in Fanon's *Black Skins, White Masks* when he describes the experience of being photographed:

> when I discover myself in the product of this operation, what I see is that I have become Total-Image, which is to say, Death-in-person; others – the Other

– do not dispossess me of myself, they turn me, fero-
ciously, into an object, they put me at their mercy, at
their disposal, classified in a file, ready for the subtlest
deceptions.[54]

Living in the United States of America, and, more than that,
in the historic seat of the confederacy, made me differently
and acutely aware of that mark that Barthes describes here,
and of the utterly irreversible and lethal consequences it
might visit upon me at any moment. Trayvon Martin's murder reminded me of it, although I arrived with the memory of
Amadou Diallo fresh in my mind from decades past, so I was
already haunted by its threat. Part of what Moten helped to
clarify for me was all the ways that I had been haunted by
these ghosts before I'd even arrived in the US, and how they
were embedded in me physically in certain crucial and complicated ways.

But there's something quite potent about trying to embrace
the kind of relationship to temporality and embodiment
that can issue from the condition of this kind of threat: the
kinetic webs of affectability that make a social world of dis-
parate bodies, and the way that that web can be materialised
in the witness of anti-Black violence. I'm thinking specifically here of Frederick Douglass's description of the murder
of the slave Demby by the overseer Mr. Gore in *Narrative of
the Life of Frederick Douglass, an American Slave, Written by Himself*. Demby refuses to submit to a bloody whipping, and after
three times refusing to accede to his own torture, has his head
shot clean from his body by musket fire in a viciously spectacular exercise of white supremacist force. Douglass writes
that, in the wake of this exhibitionist act of slaughter, '[a] thrill
of horror flashed through every soul upon the plantation,
excepting Mr. Gore. He alone seemed cool and collected.'[55]

Moten's reading of the funereal image of Emmett Till
in 'Black Mo'nin'' manifests this potency so compellingly,
and for me articulates the present-ness of pasts, the generative connections that can be forged precisely *through* lack
(just like the photograph), the power of a kind of holding on
that requires a willingness to give totally away (just like the
photograph).

50   James Baldwin, *The Evidence of Things Not Seen* (New York: Holt, Rinehart & Winston, 1985), p. 49.

51   Ibid.

52   Walter Benjamin, 'Theses on the Philosophy of History', *Illuminations* ed. by Hannah Arendt, trans. by Harry Zohn (Boston: Mariner Books, 1940, p. 198.

53   Fred Moten, 'Black Mo'nin'', *Loss: The Politics of Mourning*, ed. by David Eng and David Kazanjian (Berkeley: University of California Press, 2003), pp. 59–76.

54   Barthes, *Camera Lucida*, p. 14.

55   Frederick Douglass, *Narrative of the Life of Frederick Douglass* (Cambridge: The Belknap Press of Harvard University Press, 2009) p. 35.

Seeing, contingency, and embodiment

DC: I am mindful of the unpredictable ways that photographic projects find renewed significance and unexpected audiences over time. In February of 2020, I curated a biennial in Germany. I presented at the Kunsthalle Mannheim several images from George Georgiou's *Americans Parade*, a series of informal group portraits made at street parades across the US in the run-up to what became Trump's successful election in 2016. This was in the context of a group show about the complex legacy of the photographer Walker Evans (1903–75).[56] Georgiou's attentive observations extend Evans's fascination with the depiction of anonymous groups and individuals in public space. In October 2020, I was able to present them again at the International Center of Photography in New York, just before the election Trump was to lose and then contest with violent consequences. Any number of layers of significance in the photographs came to the fore, in ways that were powerful but also difficult to define. Everything from social distancing and collective presence, to the relations of Black, Brown, and white bodies to public space and visibility, to the temporal and psychical challenges of engaging with images as traces of a past, as uncanny premonitions, and as unexpected reactivations. For all kinds of reasons photography is particularly susceptible to this reframing and recontextualising.

George Georgiou, *Mardi Gras parade, Algiers, New Orleans, Louisiana*, 2016, from *Americans Parade* (2020)

SW-W: It's funny because I was re-reading a conversation between you and Victor Burgin recently, and he talks there about his suspicion of the claims to indexicality made on the basis of the photographic image alone, and says 'I never considered traditional photography to be indexical in any epistemologically fundamental way'. His point, as he goes on to state it against the claims of the photograph's indexical force, is that 'the image is never enough. At some point someone has to step forward and say: "I was there, I saw this" – and then even this statement has to be interrogated and either substantiated or denied by others.'[57]

I say it's funny because I think that George Georgiou's concatenated crowd images address the fraught intersections between what we see, what we *say* we see, and what's *evidenced* by seeing and imaging in some important ways. They're images of people who have gone out *to see*, or who have through some turn of events elected to stand at a threshold and gaze at the choreographed passage of people along a street as players on a stage. Very often, the bare presence of participants in the parade constitutes the event and its value ('you were there! I saw you!') And yet, the meaning of that presence is strangely uninflected as a mere visual fact.

Instead of an image of human presence clarifying its deeper meanings, a whole suite of extra-visual things that precede and encircle the visual scene need to act to give that bare presence its proper significance: where and when the parade occurs, whom it involves and addresses, which histories it marks. And then we come along, as viewers of George's images, and we see not the scene that the crowd witnesses but *their seeing*, and their vastly differentiated engagements with the scene. But part of our photographic seeing of their spectatorship means attending to difference as constitutive not just of the crowd – which is thrillingly described in gorgeous detail – but constitutive of the 'event' and of the image.

George's photographs dramatise the fact of a multiplicity of events simultaneously occurring under the umbrella of a single event (e.g., Mardi Gras) in a single frame. His frames unfold from the literal site of the event, but at instants where the attention of the audience is trained on an elsewhere: it's already happening, we can see that in their seeing, we can intuit that 'it' occurs because of their witness, but *what* occurs is so fractal and contingent and mutable and intersubjective that these singular terms – event, scene, document – seem wholly insufficient as descriptions for what is transpiring in each fraction of a second as the images unspool through the accordion structure of his book. And this is where, whether perceptibly or imperceptibly, we're called upon to 'step forward' and speak, to come back to Burgin. We have to make choices in order to see what's in front of us as fact. George's parade photographs somehow narrate that quandary, but they also make it feel like a gift. I think they leave us fruitfully at that precipice where we have to wrestle with what we declare to be happening based on what we say we can see.

DC: As we exchange these words, the International Center of Photography is installing 'But Still, It Turns', a group show curated by the photographer Paul Graham.[58] You are participating in this show, and you have taken on the most challenging element of the gallery space – a giant, square, double-height 33 ft wall. Can you say a little about how you have gone about this?

SW-W: I think that my approach to the giant wall at ICP was to try to animate the reality of how contingent and embodied perception is, and to make the movement of a viewer's body through space the central element in the constitution of whatever meaning(s) they might derive from the work. I chose to print images in vastly differing sizes (from 57 x 72 in. down to 5 x 7 in.) and I chose to arrange them so that no single monocular view-

John Halpern, installation view of 'But Still it Turns', International Center of Photography, New York (2021)

point affords you with the ability to see all of the work on the wall at once. Some images are recessed inside a vitrine protruding from the wall, others are suspended 12 to 15 ft to 25 ft from the ground, but fully recessed inside very deep box frames under mattes, so that you have to step quite far back from the wall to read the full image, while others are floated to the front of shallow frames and hung at eye level.

The wall is spectacular and imposing and monolithic, and I felt that I needed to accept that it demanded that I use scale, and that I produce images that can in some ways resolve quite easily around a readily identifiable visual figure. But I also felt that I needed to reject a Stone Mountain approach to the monolith, and to make the wall a surface for a spectator to approach and retreat from, perhaps even to circumnavigate in order to engage each of the images on legible terms.[59] If you're interested to see an image that's unclear from one point, you'll have to move, and in moving you'll surrender what's immediately legible in order to see what's unfamiliar. So the question of how fixed the photographic meanings are is unsettled by the work's presentation (hopefully), as is the question of how everything fits together. But equally, to come again back to Burgin, the works hopefully call for an interpretive response from the viewer in order to establish whatever it is that they index.

The wall is capped by an appropriated archival photograph of a young muscled white man in skimpy trunks stood on a wooden floor under bright lights in a photography studio giving a salute that resembles the crowning gesture of a gymnast's floor routine, but that also very closely resembles the Nazi salute. This final image is hung perpendicular to the wall, so it is only legible as an image if a viewer ascends to the second story. In that sense it marks a conclusion, but also potentially a beginning for a viewer who first interacts with the works upstairs. It's the largest print on the wall, and it takes on a totemic role, which seemed important in relationship with that wall, but also in relationship to the work and to the longer historical moment of its making.

Of course I didn't anticipate the assault on the US Capitol when I first found and worked with this image, but equally such gestures and such white masculinist symbolism have always been infused with a certain unilateral martial threat that's absolutist, so it's not altogether surprising that it feels apt to this moment. How it'll age, or how it'll be received, is an interesting question to consider. Paul Graham's *New Europe* is among my very favourite books, and his eradicated Hitler image, and the saluting figurine in the shop

Stanley Wolukau-Wanambwa, *Untitled*, from the series *All My Gone Life* (2014–16)

De inflatie leidde tot hamsteren en voedsel-schaar- ste: een lange rij voor een Berlijnse bakker.

The inflation led to hoarding and food short- ages: a long line at a Ber- lin baker's.

Adolf Hitler aan het begin van zijn politieke carrière. Hier spreekt hij, nog in burger, partijgenoten toe tijdens de eerste zoge- naamde vlag-inwijding

Adolf Hitler at the be- ginning of his political career. Here, still in civil- ian attire, he is address- ing fellow party members during the first so-called consecration of the flag (Munich,

Paul Graham, *Erased Hitler, Holland, 1989*, from *New Europe* (1993)

window were important touchpoints in my own development as an artist, so there's something reciprocal in the fact
that this image debuts in exhibition in a show that Graham
has curated.[60]

56 'Walker Evans Revisited', curated by David Campany, Kunsthalle Mannheim, Germany,
February – September 2020.

57 David Campany, 'Other Criteria: conversation with Victor Burgin', *Frieze*, 155 (17 May
2013) <https://www.frieze.com/article/other-criteria>

58 'But Still, It Turns' curated by Paul Graham, The International Center of Photography,
New York (February–August 2021).

59 See: Debra McKinney, 'Stone Mountain: A Monumental Dilemma', *Intelligence Report*,
Spring 2018, <https://www.splcenter.org/fighting-hate/intelligence-report/2018/
stone-mountain-monumental-dilemma>

60 Paul Graham, *New Europe* (Manchester: Fotomuseum Winterthur/Cornerhouse Publications, 1993).

Against the spectacular

DC: The multiple voices and discourses of your book find a correlative form in an installation that cannot be taken in – physically or interpretively – from any one position. It reminds me somewhat of Hans Holbein's painting *The Ambassadors* (1533), which hangs in the National Gallery, London. Standing square to it, the realism seems to offer the promise of an optimal, privileged view of these privileged men, but a skull, painted anamorphically across the bottom of the picture, beckons one to view it from the side. There is no master position, and that itself undercuts the spectacle of the painting, or shifts the spectacle into a realm of embodied engagement rather than external contemplation.

A few years ago, I curated a survey of Victor Burgin's work, at the cavernous Ambika P3 gallery in London. A rough, industrial space, over fifty feet high in places, not unlike the Turbine Hall at Tate Modern. The venue had a reputation for grandiose installations. Burgin and I conspired to ignore the scale altogether and in fact build a set of spaces for his works that was noticeably low and lateral, against expectation and monumentality. We devised a lighting system that illuminated only the walls, so all that volume of space above was plunged into darkness, and ignored, although you could sense it acoustically.

Installation view of Victor Burgin, 'A Sense of Place', Ambika P3, London (2013)

Spectacle has been the passport with which contemporary art has entered into consumer society: the museum visit as 'experience'; the museum that thinks it must cater to *everyone at all times* rather than simply being welcoming to *anyone*; the temptation to show work that's going to play well as social media publicity. The difficulty, as always, is to engage with an audience on the basis that the exhibition is 'an occasion for interpretation', to borrow an expression from Burgin, rather than a passive opportunity to receive experiences and messages, however well-intended they may be.

At the biennial I mentioned earlier, the intention was to minimise the amount of institutional text mediating the work (text that was a constitutive part of any work was a different matter). One of the shows, *Yesterday's News Today*, included a room installation that you made. The show brought together work by several artists who are reconsidering old press photos in one way or another (Thomas Ruff, Sebastian Riemer, Clare Strand). Although all the work in the biennial was visually striking and carried its richness and possibility at the visual level, I was a little nervous that audiences might hunger for 'explanation', since this is what museums routinely and rotely provide, and what audiences have come to expect. In reality, visitors were overwhelmingly happy to have the freedom to respond for themselves, without any prescriptive guide. That was extremely heartening. There is a willingness, an appetite, for open encounters in which the viewer knows, feels, that their active freedom to respond is, in the end, more important to them, and perhaps more radically important for culture, than any pre-packaged or pre-mediated message or experience. At the ICP, I'm sure your refusal of easy monumentality will startle some, and momentarily baffle others, but that's a small price to pay for the gift of such an 'occasion for interpretation'.

SW-W: I hope so. I think that for me one central point of intersection between my love of the photographic book and of installation as a grammar for embodied encounters with images is this notion of reading. I have the feeling that my resistance to the normative prescription that photographs are reducible to single meanings, and to the presumption that they are quickly and stably intelligible, also plays a role here. If spectacle has, as you say, been the passport for fine art exhibition, then installation holds out the possibility of an interruptive and deflectionary, even contradictory approach that forestalls the steady momentum of singularising readings of images. Books, of course, can do this too – differently, but effectively. Both forms can generate at least the conditions of possibility for someone to become aware of their own intellection and sensation, and of the varying and unstable connections to the objects they're faced with, hopefully in ways that are enriching. This doesn't necessarily mean fun, but it doesn't imply suffering either.

Spectacle's need to disguise and reduce relations between people down to relations between things is a singularising one, and I think that in times of sustained, epochal crisis it is often hard to persuade oneself, or others, of the virtues of the instability that comes from embracing *both/and* over and against *either/or*. The open endedness, added to the contingency, can make the prospect of indefinition terrifying, or maybe even grossly over-indulgent. But I suspect that I'm deeply attached to this sort of ethos not merely as someone who wants to write about or write with images, but also because the experience of racial difference (and all that that difference *veils* of other differences) has taught me a lot about plurality, and about the imprecise nature of our terms in relationship to the facts that they try to circumscribe. I like Darby English's arguments in *To Describe a Life* very much, especially his unswerving commitment 'to bring attention to the coincidence of contrasting phenomena, events that at once elucidate and obscure the contrasts one is exploring'.[61] The disposition to do that feeling and thinking publicly, in the moment, and to share in a process of working through it with others matters so much more than whatever conclusions one might derive.

61   Darby English, 'Introduction', *To Describe a Life: Notes from the Intersection of Art and Race Terror* (New Haven: Yale University Press, 2019), p. 21.

INCONCLUSION

It is perhaps inevitable that a conversation that turned out to revolve around questions of indeterminacy has given rise to few simple answers, and fewer clear paths forward. Making sense of photography, in its effects and affects, means attending both to its indeterminacy and its social determinants. And yes, with all the suffering and fun that might entail. Our exchanges have clarified and underscored why it is that indeterminacy, particularly as it relates to the photographic image, is to be embraced, cherished even, and not feared or disavowed. Indeterminacy is not quite the same as ambiguity, or mystery, or enigma, or even open-endedness. Rather, it signals a state of potential; a raw condition of susceptibility that is a condition of photography, although it is easily occluded by the various forces that may want to claim it, tame it, put it to work, foreclose it. Against those forces, the image can be kept indeterminate, the doors held open, if only provisionally, to admit possibility – the possibility of those differing experiences, together.

Image credits

12   Still from Kimberly Jones, 'How can we win?', 31 May 2020 © David Jones Media
        <https://www.youtube.com/watch?v=llci8MVh8J4>

14   Thomas Prior, *Untitled, New York City*, 2020, from *Amen Break* (2020). Courtesy of the artist.

15   Cover of Michael C. Dawson, *Behind the Mule: Race and Class in African-American Politics*
        (Princeton University Press, 1995).

18   Cover of Tina M. Campt, *Listening to Images* (Duke University Press, 2017).

19   Tumblr user ejmartinez, image from 'If They Gunned Me Down', Tumblr
        <https://iftheygunnedmedown.tumblr.com/post/95025909010/
        ejmartinez-iftheygunnedmedown-which-photo>

25   Spreads from *Diane Arbus: An Aperture Monograph* (Aperture, 1972) and *Deana Lawson: An
        Aperture Monograph* (Aperture, 2018).

29   Paul Strand, *Rebecca*, 1922. © Paul Strand Archive/Aperture Foundation; Paul Strand,
        Blind Woman, New York, 1916. © Paul Strand Archive/Aperture Foundation.

30   Stanley Wolukau-Wanambwa, *Officer Earl Miller, posing with the revolver used in the suicide of
        sixteen year-old Peter Lo Dolce, a student of Lane Tech, in the apartment of his fifteen year old classmate,
        Carmen Salanir, on June 24th 1951, Chicago, IL* from the series *All My Gone Life* (2014–16).

31   Stanley Wolukau-Wanambwa, *W. Baker Street*, 2014, from *Our Present Invention* (2012–14).

32–33   Helmar Lerski, *Metamorphosis 571*, *Metamorphosis 592*, *Metamorphosis 551*, *Metamorphosis
        572*, *Metamorphosis 612*, from the series *Metamorphosis through Light*, Tel Aviv, 1936, gelatin
        silver print, printed ca. 1936, 29.1 x 22.9 cm. © Estate Helmar Lerski, Fotografische
        Sammlung, Museum Folkwang, Essen / Courtesy Kicken Berlin.

35   Spreads from Gordon Parks and Ralph Ellison, 'A Man Becomes Invisible', *Life*, 25
        August 1952.

36   Jeff Wall, *After "Invisible Man" by Ralph Ellison, the Prologue*, 1999–2000, transparency in
        lightbox, 174.0 x 250.5 cm. Courtesy of the artist.

38   Stanley Wolukau-Wanambwa, *Armed Woman Shot by Police, Chicago (1957)*, from *All My Gone Life*
        (2014–16).

42   Still from Kendrick Lamar, 'Alright' (2015). Directed by Colin Tilley. <https://www.you-
        tube.com/watch?v=Z-48u_uWMHY>

44   Bill Clark, *Black Lives Matter Plaza*, 5 June 2020. © Bill Clark/CQ-Roll Call Inc.

46   Still from Flying Lotus, 'Until the Quiet Comes' (2012). Directed by Kahlil Joseph.
        <https://www.youtube.com/watch?v=-pVHC1DXQ7U>

48–49   Rabih Mroué, *The Fall of a Hair: Blow Ups*, 2012. Courtesy of the artist.

50   Sean Gallup, 'People attend a protest rally against racism following the recent death of
        George Floyd in the USA on May 31, 2020 in Berlin, Germany.' © Sean Gallup/Getty
        Images.

53   Shawn M. Pridgen, 'Power to the People - Chi Ossé on the steps of the Brooklyn Public
        Library main branch. New York, June 5, 2020.' Courtesy of the artist.

54   Kesh Nthamba, 'Racial Abuse and Police Brutality, Kibra, Kamukunji. A mural depicts
        George Floyd. In Kenya, thousands have died at the hands of the police. Police brutality
        has long been a social issue needing attention. Officers guilty of these crimes are never
        held accountable, introducing yet another grave concern of the impunity lurking deep in
        Kenya's judicial system', 3 June 2020. Courtesy of the artist.

60   Man Ray, *Dust Breeding*, 1920, printed 1964. © Man Ray 2015 Trust / DACS, London
        © Association Marcel Duchamp / ADAGP, Paris and DACS, London 2022.

61   Sophie Ristelhueber, *Because of The Dust Breeding* (1991–2007), black and white photograph/pigment print, 155 x 190cm, 1992/2007.

66   Martin Argyroglo, installation views from 'a Handful of Dust: from the Cosmic to the Domestic', Le Bal, Paris, September 2015–January 2016.

68   Spread from Walker Evans, 'Color Accidents', *Architectural Forum*, January 1958.

70   Photographer unknown, 'ACME Agency School children blow 26 days of dust from their books as striking teachers return to work', 23 March 1948. Press print.

79   Stanley Wolukau-Wanambwa, *Hermitage Rd*, 2014, from the series *All My Gone Life* (2014–16).

80   Stanley Wolukau-Wanambwa, *S. Sycamore Street*, 2014, from the series *All My Gone Life* (2014–16).

87   George Georgiou, *Mardi Gras parade, Algiers, New Orleans, Louisiana*, 6 February 2016, from *Americans Parade* (BB Editions, 2020). Courtesy of George Georgiou.

89   John Halpern, installation view of 'But Still it Turns: Recent Photography from the World', International Center of Photography, New York, 4 February–29 August 2021. © International Center of Photography, New York.

90   Stanley Wolukau-Wanambwa, *Untitled*, from the series *All My Gone Life* (2014–16).

91   Paul Graham, *Erased Hitler, Holland, 1989*, from *New Europe* (1993) © Paul Graham. Courtesy of the artist.

93   Installation view, Victor Burgin, 'A Sense of Place', Ambika P3, London, 31 October–1 December 2013. Curated by David Campany.

Much of this exchange took place in the depths of a pandemic that strained my personal and professional life, at times almost to breaking point. Alongside Stanley, there were others whose words and conversation sustained me. Sara Ickow, Dillon Gold-schlag, Jacque Donaldson, Anastasia Samoylova, Mark Neville, Lesley Martin, Elizabeth Bick, Victor Burgin. Overseeing *#ICP-Concerned*, an exhibition of work by 820 photographers from around the world, made during the nightmare of 2020, gave me purpose and perspective. Seeing and hanging every one of those images in the galleries of the International Center of Photography provided the nourishment and urgency from which a lot of my thinking in this book emerged. My thanks to them all.

David Campany

In *Why People Photograph*, Robert Adams famously wrote: 'Your own photography is never enough. Every photographer who has lasted has depended on other people's pictures too – photo-graphs that may be public or private, serious or funny, but that carry with them a reminder of community.' I hope that our book shows how true this claim has proved to be. My thanks to those who insisted on finding ways to reach out across our separate silos these last two years: Emma, David, Matthew, Vivian, Leslie, Patty, Suzanne, Lesley, Emanuel, Rhea, Saman-tha, Andrew, Shane, Remi, Daniel, Shannon, Adam, Paul, and Phil. My thanks also to Michael Mack for making space for critical and speculative experiments with the image, and to Morgan, Jess, and Louis, for your indefatigable support.

Stanley Wolukau-Wanambwa

Also from this series

DISCOURSE 001 Sally Stein *Migrant Mother, Migrant Gender*

DISCOURSE 002 Duncan Forbes *An Interview with Lewis Baltz*

DISCOURSE 003 Jörg Colberg *Photography's Neoliberal Realism*

DISCOURSE 004 C. Fausto Cabrera & Alec Soth *The Parameters of Our Cage*

DISCOURSE 005 Anna Ostoya & Chantal Mouffe *Politics and Passions*

DISCOURSE 007 Anouchka Grose & Robert Brewer Young
Uneasy Listening: Notes on Hearing and Being Heard

Indeterminacy: Thoughts on Time, the Image, and Race(ism)
David Campany & Stanley Wolukau-Wanambwa

First edition published by MACK
© 2022 MACK for this edition
© 2022 David Campany & Stanley Wolukau-Wanambwa
 for their texts

Designed by Morgan Crowcroft-Brown
Edited by Jess Gough & Louis Rogers
Printed in Germany

ISBN 978-1-913620-48-6
mackbooks.co.uk